March, 1984

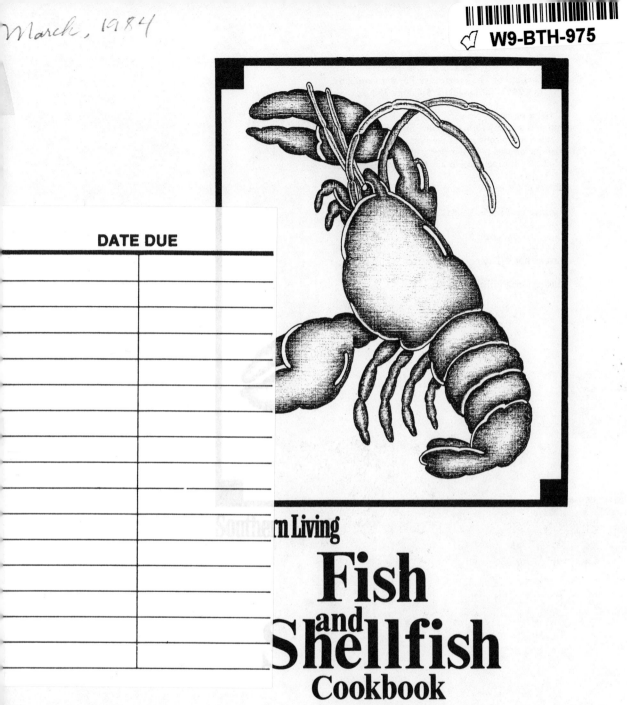

Southern Living

Fish
and
Shellfish
Cookbook

By Lena E. Sturges

Foods Editor

Library of Congress Catalog Card Number: 74–79231

Manufactured in the United States of America

Third Printing 1983

Cover Photo: Taylor Lewis

Illustration: Phillip Collier

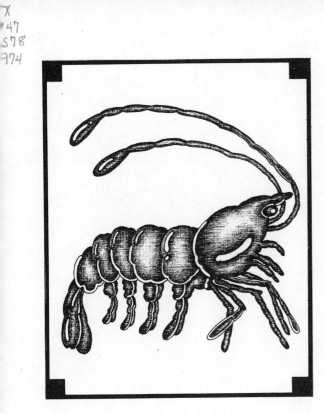

INTRODUCTION

Fresh fish and shellfish are favored entrées on the menus of Southern restaurants, and they are equally popular in home kitchens. With the myriad lakes and rivers, and the Gulf furnishing a long coastline for fishing, a fresh catch is economical as well as enjoyable.

Many varieties of fresh fish and shellfish are indigenous to the Southland, but with modern refrigeration methods, fresh fish and shellfish can be shipped to any part of the country.

Those who do not fish, take heart, for with these recipes and the availability of fish and shellfish, the bounties of the waters may be readily brought to the home table.

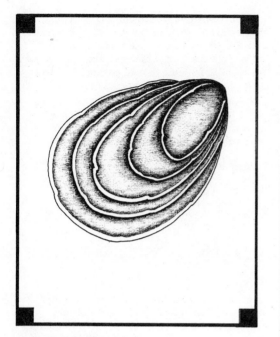

CLAMS

Because the clam has been established in our minds as a chowder ingredient, many people do not realize the wide variety of other dishes which can be prepared with this popular shellfish. Like oysters, they are also enjoyed raw.

Clams may be purchased fresh, canned, or frozen (already prepared by various methods) in most supermarkets.

As is true with most shellfish, clams require a short cooking time. In fact, most people consider a "well-cooked" clam a "clam-ity."

VENUS CLAM DIP

2½ pounds minced clams, fresh or frozen
¾ cup chopped onion
¼ cup chopped green pepper
½ cup butter or margarine
3 tablespoons all-purpose flour
¼ teaspoon salt
⅛ teaspoon pepper
1 cup reserved clam liquor
1 cup shredded pasteurized process American cheese
1 (8-ounce) jar pasteurized process cheese spread
2 tablespoons chopped pimiento
¼ cup chili sauce
1 teaspoon Worcestershire sauce
½ teaspoon hot pepper sauce
Corn chips

Thaw clams if frozen. Cook in natural liquor for 4 to 5 minutes, or until clams are done. Drain. Reserve liquor. Sauté onion and green pepper in butter until tender. Blend in flour, salt, and pepper. Add reserved clam liquor gradually and cook over moderate heat until sauce is thick, stirring constantly. Add shredded cheese and cheese spread and continue to heat until cheese melts. Add pimiento, chili sauce, Worcestershire sauce, hot pepper sauce, and clams. Heat. Serve hot with corn chips. Yield: 4½ cups dip.

CLAMS CASINO

3 green peppers, chopped
2 ribs celery, chopped
1 onion, chopped
½ cup butter or margarine
½ cup clam liquor
1 (4-ounce) jar pimientos, chopped
Salt, pepper, Worcestershire sauce, and hot pepper sauce to taste
12 clams on half-shell
Rock salt
2 slices bacon, cooked crisp and crumbled

Sauté peppers, celery, and onion in butter. Add clam liquor and cook until liquid is reduced by half. Add pimientos, and season with salt, pepper, Worcestershire sauce, and hot pepper sauce. Arrange clams on the half shell on a bed of rock salt in a flat pan. Cover clams with cooked mixture, and top with crumbled bacon. Bake at 400° for about 8 minutes. Yield: 4 to 6 servings.

BROILED CLAM CANAPES

- 1 (8-ounce) can minced clams
- 1 (3-ounce) package chive cream cheese
- 1 tablespoon freshly squeezed lemon juice
- ½ teaspoon salt
- 3 drops hot pepper sauce
- 1 egg white
  Crackers or toast
  Paprika

Drain clams. Soften cheese to room temperature. Combine cheese, lemon juice, seasonings, and clams. Fold into stiffly beaten egg white. Spread on crackers or toast; sprinkle with paprika. Place on broiler pan about 3 inches from source of heat. Broil 2 to 3 minutes, or until brown. Serve at once. Yield: 36 canapés.

CLAM AND CORN CHOWDER

- 1 pint clams
- ¼ cup chopped bacon
- 1 cup chopped onion
- 1 cup clam liquor and water
- 1 cup diced potatoes
- 1 teaspoon celery salt
- 1 teaspoon salt
  Dash pepper
- 1 cup cooked or canned whole kernel corn
- 2 cups milk
- 1 tablespoon butter or margarine
- ⅓ cup cracker crumbs

Drain clams and save liquor. Chop. Fry bacon until crisp; drain on absorbent paper. Sauté onion in bacon drippings until tender. Add clam liquor and water, potatoes, seasonings, and clams. Cook for about 15 minutes, or until potatoes are tender. Add corn, milk, and butter; heat. Stir in crumbs. Garnish with bacon sprinkled over the top. Yield: 6 servings.

MANHATTAN CLAM CHOWDER

- 1 pint clams
- ¼ cup chopped bacon
- ½ cup chopped onion
- ½ cup chopped green pepper
- 1 cup chopped celery
- 1 cup clam liquor and water
- 1 cup diced potatoes
- ¼ teaspoon thyme
- 1 teaspoon salt
  Dash cayenne pepper
- 2 cups tomato juice

Drain clams and save liquor. Chop. Fry bacon until lightly brown. Add onion, green pepper, and celery; cook until tender. Add clam liquor and water, potatoes, clam seasonings, and clams. Cook for about 15 minutes, or until potatoes are tender. Add tomato juice; heat. Serve hot. Yield: 6 servings.

NEW ENGLAND CLAM CHOWDER

- 1 pint clams
- ¼ cup chopped bacon
- ¼ cup chopped onion
- 1 cup clam liquor and water
- 1 cup diced potatoes
- ½ teaspoon salt
  Dash pepper
- 2 cups milk
  Chopped parsley

Drain clams and save liquor. Chop. Fry bacon until lightly brown. Add onion and sauté until tender. Add clam liquor and water, potatoes, seasonings, and clams. Cook for about 15 minutes, or until potatoes are tender. Add milk; heat. Garnish with chopped parsley sprinkled over the top. Serve hot. Yield: 6 servings.

DEVILED CLAMS

- 1 pint shucked clams
- 3 tablespoons butter or margarine
- 1 small clove garlic, minced
- 1 tablespoon chopped onion
- 1 tablespoon finely chopped green pepper
- ½ cup finely chopped celery
- 2 tablespoons all-purpose flour
- ½ teaspoon salt
- ⅛ teaspoon pepper
- ⅛ teaspoon dried thyme leaves
- ½ cup clam liquor
- 3 drops hot pepper sauce
- 1 tablespoon chili sauce
- 1 egg, slightly beaten
- 1 tablespoon dried parsley flakes
- ¼ cup cracker meal
- 16 clam shells
- 2 tablespoons melted butter or margarine
- ½ cup fine dry bread crumbs

Drain clams and reserve liquor; chop clams. Melt butter in a saucepan; add garlic, onion, green pepper, and celery. Cook until tender. Blend in flour, salt, pepper, and thyme. Gradually add the ½ cup reserved clam liquor, hot pepper sauce, chili sauce, and clams; cook over moderate heat, stirring constantly, until thickened. Stir a little of the clam mixture into beaten egg; add to remaining clam mixture and blend well. Stir in parsley and cracker meal. Spoon into clam shells or individual casserole dishes. Mix melted butter and bread crumbs and sprinkle over clam mixture. Bake at 400° for 12 to 15 minutes, or until crumbs are lightly browned. Yield: 4 servings.

CLAM AND CHEESE DIP

    1 (8-ounce) can minced clams
    2 (3-ounce) packages cream cheese
    2 teaspoons grated onion
    2 teaspoons freshly squeezed lemon juice
    1 teaspoon Worcestershire sauce
    1 teaspoon chopped parsley
    ¼ teaspoon salt
    3 drops hot pepper sauce
      Canned whole cranberries

Drain clams and save liquor. Soften cheese to room temperature. Combine all ingredients except cranberries and liquor; blend into a paste. Gradually add about ¼ cup clam liquor and beat until mixture has consistency of whipped cream. Chill. Serve in a bowl. Garnish with cranberries. Yield: about 1 pint of dip.

CLAM SURPRISE

    2 eggs, well beaten
    1 teaspoon horseradish
    2 dozen shucked soft-shell clams (about 1 cup)
    2 dozen small spinach leaves
    1 cup all-purpose flour
      Shortening or salad oil for frying

Beat eggs; add horseradish. Take clams and wrap each with a spinach leaf; dip each clam into egg mixture, and then dip lightly into flour. Heat shortening to 350° in a frying pan. Put clams in pan; fry until golden brown. Remove and serve hot. Yield: 4 servings.

STEAMED CLAMS

Scrub shells thoroughly; rinse well. Remove sand from the "neck" of large clams (split with scissors and press out sand; rinse thoroughly). Place clams on rack in large kettle with a tight-fitting cover; add ½ cup boiling water for each gallon of clams. Cover; steam until shells are partially open, about 8 to 10 minutes. Do not overcook. Serve very hot with a side dish of melted butter; allow 15 to 25 clams per person.

DEEP-FRIED CLAMS

    1 quart clams
    1 egg, beaten
    1 tablespoon milk
    1 teaspoon salt
      Dash pepper
    1 cup dry bread crumbs or cracker crumbs
      Shortening

Drain clams. Combine egg, milk, and seasonings. Dip clams in egg mixture and roll in crumbs. Deep-fry in a basket in shortening at 375° for 2 to 3 minutes, or until brown. Drain on absorbent paper. Serve plain or with a sauce. Yield: 6 servings.

CLAM FRITTERS

    1 pint clams
    1¾ cups all-purpose flour
    1 tablespoon baking powder
    ½ teaspoon ground nutmeg
    1½ teaspoons salt
    2 eggs, beaten
    1 cup milk
    2 teaspoons grated onion
    1 tablespoon butter or margarine, melted

Drain clams and chop. Combine dry ingredients. Combine eggs, milk, onion, butter, and clams. Combine with dry ingredients and stir until smooth. Drop batter by teaspoonsful into hot shortening at 350° and fry for 3 minutes, or until golden brown. Drain on absorbent paper. Yield: 6 servings.

FRIED CLAMS

    1 quart clams, drained
    1 egg, beaten
    1 tablespoon milk
    1 teaspoon salt
      Dash pepper
    1 cup dry bread crumbs or cracker crumbs
      Shortening

Drain clams. Combine egg, milk, and seasonings. Dip clams in egg mixture and roll in crumbs. Place clams in a heavy frying pan which contains about ⅛ inch of shortening, hot but not smoking. Fry at moderate heat. When clams are brown on one side, turn carefully and brown on other side for 5 to 8 minutes. Drain on absorbent paper. Yield: 6 servings.

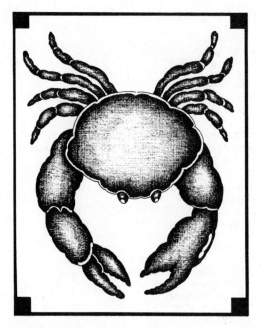

CRABS

In the shallow waters of bays, sounds, and channels scattered along the Atlantic coast from Massachusetts to Texas, travelers from inland areas have sometimes observed an unusual sight. A child attaches a large piece of meat to a string, drops it into the water, and jerks up a large crab whose pincers are clamped to the meat. The crab is secured by another child standing by with a net.

Actually, when one considers what savory dishes crabs make, it is no wonder that the sport is as profitable as it is fun. The crab is caught and marketed in both the hard-shelled and soft-shelled stages. Soft-shelled crabs especially are considered delicacies. What exactly is a soft-shelled crab? First, it is important to understand that the young crab sheds (or molts) about 15 times before reaching maturity (during their second summer). When the shell splits and the crab backs out of it, soft-shelled crab fishermen are alert to this change. They watch for the color of the crab to turn red. At this point, the crab (called a "buster") is ready to emerge from the shell. This shedding takes about 2 or 3 hours. Within 9 to 12 hours, the outer skin is paper-thin and at this stage the crab is known as a soft-shelled crab. After a short cooking period, the entire body can be eaten. Frying is the preferred cooking method.

Crab fanciers should keep one other thing in mind. When crabmeat is purchased, whether blue crab or Alaskan King crab, it should be refrigerated until ready for use.

CRAB A LA KING

1 pound cooked crabmeat
1 cup finely chopped celery
½ green pepper, finely chopped
1 pint heavy cream
2 hard-cooked eggs, chopped
1 tablespoon melted butter
1 tablespoon Worcestershire sauce
   Salt and pepper to taste
3 tablespoons sherry

Remove any shell and cartilage from crabmeat. Simmer celery and green pepper in a double boiler with a little water until tender. Drain, add cream, crabmeat, eggs, butter, and seasonings. Simmer only until heated through. Add sherry just before serving. Serve on toast. Yield: 6 servings.

CRABMEAT AU GRATIN

3 tablespoons butter or margarine
½ green pepper, minced
½ onion, chopped
3 tablespoons all-purpose flour
2 cups milk
2 cups crabmeat, shell or cartilage removed
½ teaspoon salt
   Dash ground nutmeg
½ cup shredded cheese
   Buttered bread crumbs

Melt butter; add pepper and onion and cook for 5 minutes. Add flour and milk, then crabmeat, salt, and nutmeg. Cook 10 minutes. Pour in shallow buttered baking dish or use crab shells. Sprinkle with shredded cheese and buttered bread crumbs and bake at 350° until cheese is brown. Yield: 4 to 6 servings.

SOUTHERN CRAB CAKES

1 pound crabmeat
4 tablespoons melted butter or margarine
½ teaspoon salt
¼ teaspoon black pepper
   Pinch cayenne pepper
1 tablespoon water
2 eggs, well-beaten
   Fine bread crumbs
   Salad oil

Mix crabmeat, butter, seasonings, and enough beaten eggs to mold into small cakes. Beat 1 tablespoon water into the remaining beaten eggs and dip the cakes into this mixture. Roll in crumbs. Sauté until rich brown in a heavy frying pan or fry in deep oil at 380°. Serve hot. Yield: 4 to 6 servings.

CRAB CANAPES

- 1 pound crabmeat
- 3 tablespoons mayonnaise
- 1 tablespoon prepared mustard
- ¼ teaspoon salt
  Dash pepper
- 1 tablespoon freshly squeezed lemon juce
- 12 slices white bread
- ¼ cup grated Parmesan cheese
- 2 tablespoons dry bread crumbs

Remove any shell or cartilage from crabmeat. Combine mayonnaise, seasonings, lemon juice, and crabmeat. Remove crusts and toast bread. Spread crab mixture on each slice of toast. Combine cheese and crumbs; sprinkle over top of each slice of toast. Cut each slice into 6 pieces. Place on a broiler pan about 3 inches from source of heat. Broil for 2 to 3 minutes or until brown. Yield: about 6 dozen canapés.

HOT CRAB CANAPES

- 36 slices day-old bread
- 1 cup flaked crab
- ¼ cup mayonnaise
- 1 teaspoon tarragon vinegar
- ½ teaspoon dry mustard
- ¼ teaspoon salt
  Dash pepper
- 1 tablespoon minced parsley
- 1 tablespoon minced chives
  Grated Parmesan cheese
  Paprika

Cut bread in desired shapes and toast on one side. Combine crab, mayonnaise, vinegar, seasonings, parsley, and chives. Spread crab mixture on untoasted sides of bread. Sprinkle with cheese and paprika. Place on a cookie sheet and just before serving, broil 3 inches from source of heat until brown. Yield: 3 dozen canapés.

KING CRAB CANAPES

- 1 (6½-ounce) package King crabmeat or other, fresh or frozen
- 1 (6½- or 7½-ounce) can crabmeat
- 1 (8-ounce) package flaky baking powder biscuits
- ½ cup shredded Cheddar cheese
- 2 tablespoons mayonnaise or salad dressing
- 1½ teaspoons chopped chives
- 2 drops hot pepper sauce
  Dash pepper
- ¼ teaspoon salt
- 2 egg whites

Thaw crabmeat; drain. Remove any remaining shell or cartilage. Chop the crabmeat. Separate each biscuit into two thin biscuits and place in a 15- x 10- x 1-inch baking pan. Bake at 400° for 6 to 8 minutes or until lightly browned. Remove from oven, and turn biscuits over on baking pan. Combine cheese, mayonnaise, chives, hot pepper sauce, pepper, and crabmeat. Mix thoroughly. Add salt to egg whites and beat until stiff but not dry. Fold crab mixture into egg whites. Top each biscuit with a tablespoonful of crab mixture. Bake at 450° or 8 to 10 minutes or until lightly browned. Yield: 20 canapes.

BAKED CRABMEAT IN SHELLS

- 1 pound crabmeat
- ½ cup chopped onion
- ¼ cup butter or margarine, melted
- 2 tablespoons all-purpose flour
- ½ cup milk
- ½ cup tomato sauce
- ½ teaspoon salt
  Dash pepper
- ¼ cup grated cheese
- ½ cup soft bread crumbs

Remove any shell or cartilage from crabmeat. Cook onion in butter until tender. Blend in flour. Add milk gradually and cook until thick, stirring constantly. Add tomato sauce, seasonings, and crabmeat. Place in 6 well-greased, individual shells or 5-ounce custard cups. Combine cheese and crumbs; sprinkle over top of each shell. Bake at 350° for 20 to 25 minutes or until browned. Yield: 6 servings.

CRAB DELICIOUS

- 2 pounds crabmeat, fresh or frozen, or
- 6 (6½-ounce) cans crabmeat
- ⅔ cup butter or margarine, melted
- 3 tablespoons freshly squeezed lemon juice
- ½ teaspoon salt
  Dash pepper
  Dash hot pepper sauce
  Chopped parsley

Thaw frozen crabmeat or drain canned crabmeat. Remove any remaining shell or cartilage from crabmeat. Combine all ingredients except parsley. Place in 6 well-greased, individual shells or 5-ounce custard cups. Place on a broiler pan about 4 inches from source of heat. Broil for 10 or 12 minutes or until golden brown. Garnish with chopped parsley. Yield: 6 servings.

CRAB CAKES

1 pound or 2 (6½-ounce) cans crabmeat
1 medium onion, chopped
½ cup butter or margarine
1 cup fine dry bread crumbs
3 eggs
1 teaspoon salt
1 teaspoon dry mustard
  Few sprigs parsley, finely chopped
2 tablespoons cream
  All-purpose flour

Flake crabmeat if necessary. Cook chopped onion in ¼ cup butter until limp. Add breadcrumbs and mix well.

Beat eggs thoroughly and add to crabmeat along with crumb mixture, salt, mustard, chopped parsley, and cream. Shape into 8 flat patties, coat with flour, and sauté in remaining butter until delicately browned on both sides. Yield: 4 servings.

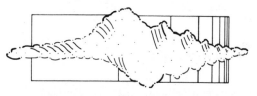

CRABMEAT-ARTICHOKE CASSEROLE

3 tablespoons butter or margarine
3 tablespoons all-purpose flour
1 teaspoon salt
⅛ teaspoon pepper
⅛ teaspoon dry mustard
1½ cups milk
½ teaspoon Worcestershire sauce
  Dash hot pepper sauce
¼ cup grated Parmesan cheese
1 pound crabmeat
1 (14-ounce) can artichoke hearts, drained
4 hard-cooked eggs, sliced
½ cup buttered bread crumbs
¼ cup grated Parmesan cheese

Melt butter; blend in flour, salt, pepper, and mustard until smooth. Gradually add milk and cook until thickened, stirring constantly. Add Worcestershire sauce, hot pepper sauce, ¼ cup Parmesan cheese, and crabmeat; mix well.

Arrange artichoke hearts in bottom of a 1½-quart casserole dish and cover with sliced eggs. Spoon in crab mixture. Top with buttered bread crumbs which have been mixed with ¼ cup Parmesan cheese. Bake at 350° for 30 to 40 minutes. Yield: 6 to 8 servings.

MARYLAND CRABMEAT CASSEROLE

¼ cup butter or margarine
3 tablespoons all-purpose flour
2 cups milk
2 tablespoons minced onion
½ teaspoon celery salt
¼ teaspoon grated orange rind
1 tablespoon chopped parsley
1 tablespoon minced green pepper
1 pimiento, minced
  Dash hot pepper sauce
1 teaspoon salt
  Dash pepper
2 tablespoons sherry
1 egg, beaten
3 cups crabmeat, drained
½ cup fresh bread crumbs
½ cup shredded sharp process cheese
3 half slices tomato

Melt butter in double boiler; stir in flour till smooth, then add milk. Cook, stirring constantly, until thickened. Add onion, celery salt, orange rind, parsley, green pepper, pimiento, hot pepper sauce, salt, and pepper.

Remove from heat; add sherry, and slowly stir some of sauce into beaten egg; stir egg mixture into rest of sauce. Remove cartilage from crabmeat, if canned. With fork, fold crabmeat into sauce. Spoon into a 1½-quart casserole dish. Toss bread crumbs with cheese. Sprinkle around top edges of casserole. Bake at 350° for 10 minutes. Arrange tomato slices down the center of casserole. Bake 5 minutes longer, or until crumbs are golden brown. Yield: 6 servings.

CRAB-RICE CASSEROLE

1 (6-ounce) package seasoned white and wild rice mix
1 large onion, finely chopped
1 large stalk green celery, chopped
2 tablespoons salad oil
1 apple, chopped
1 to 2 teaspoons curry powder
½ teaspoon Ac'cent
3 (6½-ounce) cans crabmeat, thoroughly drained
2 tablespoons seedless raisins

Cook rice according to package directions but omit butter and decrease cooking time to 20 minutes. (Rice will be moist.)

Sauté onion and celery in salad oil until onion is golden. Stir in apple, curry powder, Ac'cent, drained crabmeat, raisins, and cooked rice. Spoon into a 2-quart casserole dish; cover and bake at 375° for 20 minutes. Yield: 6 servings.

CRAB COQUILLE

½ pound cooked crabmeat
2 hard-cooked eggs, chopped
1¾ cup soft bread crumbs
1 tablespoon grated onion
1 tablespoon chopped celery
1 tablespoon chopped green pepper
1 teaspoon freshly squeezed lemon juice
½ teaspoon prepared mustard
¼ teaspoon salt
1 (10¾-ounce) can cream of chicken soup
¼ cup water
¼ cup grated Parmesan cheese

Mix crabmeat with chopped hard-cooked eggs and 1 cup bread crumbs (reserve rest of crumbs for topping). Add onion, celery, green pepper, lemon juice, mustard, and salt. Combine with soup and water to make a moist mixture. Mix lightly. Pile in 4 to 6 scallop shells or very shallow baking dish. Top with crumbs and ¼ cup grated Parmesan cheese. Bake at 400° for 15 to 20 minutes, or until brown. Yield: 4 to 6 servings.

CREAMED CRAB CUM RICE

3 tablespoons chopped green pepper
¼ cup chopped onion
2 tablespoons butter or margarine
1 (10¾-ounce) can cream of mushroom soup
1 (6½-ounce) can crabmeat
1 cup cooked rice
Chopped parsley

Sauté green pepper and onion in butter. Stir in soup and mix well. Add crabmeat and stir over low heat until thoroughly heated. Serve over hot rice and sprinkle with parsley. Yield: 2 servings.

CREAMED CRABMEAT

4 tablespoons butter or margarine
4 tablespoons all-purpose flour
1 (13¾-ounce) can chicken broth
¼ cup Sauterne
4 eggs, well beaten
4 tablespoons freshly squeezed lemon juice
1 cup crabmeat
Patty shells or toast points

Melt butter in blazer pan of chafing dish over direct heat. Stir in flour and keep stirring until smooth. Gradually add chicken broth and wine, stirring constantly until sauce is thick and smooth.

Remove from direct heat and place in top of double boiler over hot, but not boiling, water.

Beat eggs in small bowl. Add lemon juice gradually, beating constantly. Gradually beat in about a cup of the warm sauce. Slowly stir this mixture into the rest of the sauce in chafing dish; mix well. Add crabmeat, and heat. Serve in patty shells or on toast points. Yield: 4 servings.

DEVILED CRAB

1 pound crabmeat
4 hard-cooked eggs
1 tablespoon Worcestershire sauce
½ teaspoon hot pepper sauce
½ teaspoon pepper
2 cups cracker crumbs
½ cup butter or margarine, melted
12 crab shells

Break crabmeat into pieces; remove any remaining shell or cartilage. Peel and chop hard-cooked eggs. Combine with remaining ingredients and spoon into crab shells. Bake at 375° for about 10 minutes. Yield: 12 servings.

CAROLINA DEVILED CRAB

1 pound blue crabmeat, fresh or pasteurized
2 tablespoons chopped onion
2 tablespoons melted butter or margarine
2 tablespoons all-purpose flour
¾ cup milk
1 tablespoon freshly squeezed lemon juice
1½ teaspoons dry mustard
1 teaspoon Worcestershire sauce
½ teaspoon salt
3 drops hot pepper sauce
Dash black pepper
Dash cayenne pepper
1 egg, beaten
1 tablespoon chopped parsley
1 tablespoon melted butter or margarine
¼ cup dry bread crumbs

Remove any remaining shell or cartilage from crabmeat. Cock onion in butter until tender. Blend in flour. Add milk gradually and cook until thick, stirring constantly. Add lemon juice and seasonings. Stir a little of the hot sauce into the egg; add to remaining sauce, stirring constantly. Add parsley and crabmeat; blend well. Place in 6 well-greased individual shells or 5-ounce custard cups. Combine butter and crumbs; sprinkle over top of each shell. Bake at 350° for 20 to 25 minutes or until brown. Yield: 6 servings.

TOMATOES WITH CRABMEAT DRESSING

1 pound crabmeat, fresh or frozen
        or
2 (6½-ounce) cans crabmeat
1 cup grated carrot
2 hard-cooked eggs, chopped
1 tablespoon chopped onion
1 cup mayonnaise
¼ cup freshly squeezed lemon juice
1 teaspoon prepared mustard
1 teaspoon salt
¼ teaspoon pepper
18 tomato slices
6 lettuce leaves

Thaw frozen crabmeat or drain canned crabmeat. Remove any shell or cartilage from crabmeat. Combine carrot, chopped eggs, onion, and crabmeat. Combine mayonnaise, lemon juice, mustard, salt, and pepper; mix thoroughly. Add mayonnaise mixture to crab mixture; toss lightly. Chill. Arrange 3 tomato slices on each lettuce leaf; sprinkle with salt. Top tomatoes with approximately ⅔ cup crabmeat dressing. Yield: 6 servings.

CRABMEAT ELEANOR

1 (4-ounce) can button mushrooms
¼ cup slivered, blanched almonds
1 small green pepper, cut into 1-inch strips
¼ cup melted butter or margarine
2 tablespoons orange juice
1 teaspoon freshly squeezed lemon juice
2 (10¾-ounce) cans cream of mushroom soup
½ teaspoon celery salt
¼ cup quartered ripe olives
¼ cup chopped pimiento
2 tablespoons chopped parsley
    Dash hot pepper sauce
3 (3-ounce) cans crabmeat
    Salt and pepper to taste
    Hot cooked rice
    Chives

Drain mushrooms and reserve liquid. Lightly sauté mushrooms, almonds, and green pepper in melted butter. Add mushroom liquid, orange and lemon juices, mushroom soup, and celery salt. Blend well over low heat. Stir in olives, pimiento, parsley, and hot pepper sauce. Flake crabmeat and remove any shell. Add to hot mixture and season to taste with salt and pepper. Heat thoroughly, but do not boil. Hold over very low heat, if necessary, until serving time. Spoon over hot, fluffy rice tossed with chives. Yield: 8 servings.

CRABMEAT FILLING FOR CREPES

½ cup chopped green pepper
2 tablespoons butter or margarine
4 tablespoons all-purpose flour
1 cup half-and-half
1 egg yolk, beaten
1 pound crabmeat
1 cup commercial sour cream
2 tablespoons grated Romano cheese
    Salt and pepper to taste
    Hollandaise Sauce (optional)
12 crêpes

Sauté green pepper in butter. Add flour and half-and-half, stirring constantly, cooking until thick. Add a little of the hot mixture to the egg yolk; then stir back into the mixture in the saucepan. When quite thick, add crabmeat, sour cream, and cheese. Season to taste and heat to serving temperature. Spoon over crêpes and roll up. Top rolled crêpes with Hollandaise Sauce, if desired. Yield: 3½ cups.

Hollandaise Sauce

3 egg yolks
2 tablespoons freshly squeezed lemon juice
½ teaspoon salt
½ cup melted butter or margarine
½ cup boiling water

Combine egg yolks, lemon juice, salt, and butter in blender. Blend until smooth, about 5 seconds. Remove cover and gradually add boiling water as blending continues. Pour entire mixture in top of double boiler and cook over hot water, stirring constantly, until sauce is the consistency of soft custard. Remove from heat. Serve warm, or store in refrigerator and reheat as needed. Yield: 1 cup.

CRAB FONDUE

½ pound crabmeat
1 (10½-ounce) can cream of shrimp soup
¼ cup milk or half-and-half
½ cup shredded pasteurized process American or Cheddar cheese
2 teaspoons freshly squeezed lemon juice
    Dash paprika
    Dash white pepper
2 tablespoons sherry (optional)
    Melba toast
    Milk (optional)

Remove any remaining shell or cartilage from crabmeat. Combine soup with milk in fondue pot. Cover; heat over direct moderate flame, stirring frequently. Fold in remaining ingredients except sherry. Adjust heat to low flame. If desired, stir in sherry just before serving.

Use as an appetizer with melba toast or as a luncheon dish on toast points or in patty shells. Add milk if a thinner mixture is desired. Yield: approximately 2¼ cups.

CRAB IMPERIAL

1 **pound white cooked crabmeat**
1 **egg, well beaten**
½ **cup mayonnaise**
2 **tablespoons melted butter or margarine**
2 **tablespoons evaporated milk**
2 **tablespoons capers**
 Salt and pepper to taste
½ **cup grated Parmesan cheese**

Remove any remaining shell or cartilage from crabmeat, but leave it in lumps. Lightly mix it with the other ingredients, except cheese. Place in a greased 1½-quart casserole dish and sprinkle with grated cheese. Bake at 350° for 25 minutes. Yield: 6 servings.

CRABMEAT LORENZO

1 **pound crabmeat**
2 **cloves garlic, chopped**
¼ **pound butter or margarine**
½ **bunch shallots, chopped**
1 **green pepper, chopped**
1 **tablespoon all-purpose flour**
1 **cup milk**
6 **sprigs parsley, chopped**
½ **cup sherry**
1 **cup bread crumbs**
6 **crisp toast rounds**
12 **anchovy strips**
4 **tablespoons shredded Italian cheese**

Remove any remaining shell or cartilage from crabmeat. Sauté garlic in butter until half brown. Add shallots and green pepper. Cook slowly until done, but not brown. Add flour and stir in well. Add milk and parsley; stir until thick. Add sherry. Fold in crabmeat. Sprinkle in bread crumbs. Mold into balls and place on round, crisp toast. Lay 2 strips of anchovies on top of each piece of toast. Sprinkle with Italian cheese. Bake under broiler until brown. Yield: 6 servings.

CRAB LOUIS

1 **pound crabmeat**
1 **head lettuce**
½ **teaspoon salt**
1 **cucumber, sliced**
4 **tomatoes, sliced**
3 **hard-cooked eggs, sliced**
 Louis Dressing

Remove any shell or cartilage from crabmeat, being careful not to break the meat into small pieces. Shred lettuce and place in a large shallow salad bowl. Sprinkle with salt. Arrange the crabmeat over the lettuce. Around the edge place alternate slices of cucumbers, tomatoes, and eggs. Spread Louis Dressing over crabmeat. Yield: 6 servings.

Louis Dressing

1 **cup mayonnaise or salad dressing**
3 **tablespoons catsup**
2 **tablespoons chopped sweet pickle**
1 **tablespoon freshly squeezed lemon juice**

Combine all ingredients and chill. Yield: 1 cup.

CRAB MORNAY

1 **pound cooked crabmeat**
½ **cup butter or margarine**
3 **tablespoons all-purpose flour**
1 **teaspoon salt**
2 **cups milk**
½ **teaspoon white pepper**
½ **pound shredded Cheddar cheese**

Remove all shell and cartilage from crabmeat. Make a thick cream sauce of butter, flour, salt, milk, and white pepper. Put a layer of crabmeat, a layer of cheese, and some of the cream sauce in a 1½-quart casserole dish. Continue until all ingredients are used. Bake at 350° for 25 to 30 minutes. Yield: 6 servings.

CRAB MORNAY FLORENTINE

  1 pound fresh spinach, or 1 (10-ounce)
      package frozen spinach
  3 tablespoons butter or margarine
  2 tablespoons all-purpose flour
1½ cups milk
  ½ cup shredded Swiss cheese
  ½ cup light cream
     Dash cayenne pepper
  1 pound or 2 (6½-ounce) cans crabmeat
  ½ cup dry bread crumbs

Cook spinach in a little salted water until tender
(follow package directions for frozen), drain well,
and chop rather fine. Transfer to bottom of a
buttered 2-quart casserole or baking dish.

Melt 2 tablespoons butter in a saucepan; stir in
flour until smooth; add milk gradually. Cook
over a low heat, stirring constantly, until sauce
begins to thicken. Add cheese, cream, and cayenne
pepper. Cook over low heat until thick, about
10 minutes. Remove from heat and stir in
crabmeat. Pour mixture over spinach, sprinkle
with bread crumbs, and dot surface with remaining
butter. Broil about 5 minutes or until appetizingly
browned. Yield: 4 servings.

CRAB NEWBURG

  1 pound crabmeat
  ⅓ cup butter or margarine
  3 tablespoons all-purpose flour
  ½ teaspoon salt
  ½ teaspoon paprika
     Dash cayenne pepper
1½ cups half-and-half
  3 egg yolks, beaten
  2 tablespoons sherry
     Toast points

Remove any shell or cartilage from crabmeat,
being careful not to break the meat into small
pieces. Melt butter; blend in flour and seasonings.
Add half-and-half gradually and cook until thick,
stirring constantly. Stir a little of the hot sauce
into egg yolks; add to remaining sauce, stirring
constantly. Add crabmeat; heat. Remove from heat
and slowly stir in sherry. Serve immediately on
toast points. Yield: 6 servings.

HOT CRABMEAT PIE

  2 (3-ounce) packages cream cheese
  1 (6½-ounce) can crabmeat, flaked, well drained
  2 tablespoons instant minced onion
  1 tablespoon milk
  ½ teaspoon horseradish
  ¼ teaspoon salt
     Dash pepper
  ⅓ cup sliced blanched almonds

Combine cheese, crabmeat, onion, milk,
horseradish, salt, and pepper. Mix well. Spoon
mixture into a greased 8-inch pie plate; sprinkle
with almonds. Bake at 375° for 15 to 20 minutes.
Yield: 8 servings.

CRAB RAVIGOTE

  1 pound crabmeat
  2 tablespoons chopped sweet pickle
  2 tablespoons freshly squeezed lemon juice
  ¼ teaspoon salt
     Dash pepper
  1 hard-cooked egg, chopped
  1 tablespoon chopped parsley
  2 tablespoons chopped onion
  ¼ cup mayonnaise or salad dressing
  2 tablespoons chopped stuffed olives
  ¼ teaspoon paprika
     Pimiento strips

Remove any shell or cartilage from crabmeat.
Combine pickle, lemon juice, seasonings, egg,
parsley, onion, and crabmeat. Place in 6 individual
shells or on salad greens. Combine mayonnaise,
olives, and paprika; spread over top of crab
mixture. Chill. Garnish with pimiento strips.
Yield: 6 servings.

CRABMEAT ST. JACQUES

¼ onion, chopped
½ green pepper, chopped
 1 (4-ounce) can chopped mushrooms, drained
    Butter or margarine
 2 cups white sauce
    Salt and pepper
    Paprika
 1 teaspoon Worcestershire sauce
 1 pound canned crabmeat
    Shredded pasteurized process American cheese
    Buttered bread crumbs
    Paprika

Sauté onion, pepper, and mushrooms in a small amount of butter. Add the white sauce seasoned with salt and pepper, a generous amount of paprika, and Worcestershire sauce. Add crabmeat and stir to mix.

Put mixture into a greased casserole dish and sprinkle top lightly with shredded American cheese, buttered bread crumbs, and paprika. Bake at 450° for 15 minutes. Yield: 6 servings.

CRABMEAT SALAD

2 envelopes unflavored gelatin
1 cup cold water
½ teaspoon salt
  Hot pepper sauce
¼ cup freshly squeezed lemon juice
2 cups mayonnaise
2 teaspoons instant minced onion
1 cup chopped celery
2 (6½-ounce) cans crabmeat
  Salad greens
  Pimiento strips
  Crabmeat for garnish

Soften gelatin in water. Heat gently, stirring until gelatin is dissolved. Add seasonings, lemon juice, mayonnaise and onion. Beat with rotary beater until blended. Chill until slightly thickened. Fold in celery and flaked crabmeat. Pour into 5-cup fish mold or other mold and chill until firm. Unmold on greens and garnish with pimiento strips and crabmeat. Yield: 6 to 8 servings.

CRAB LUNCHEON SALAD

½ cup commercial sour cream
½ cup mayonnaise or salad dressing
1 tablespoon white wine vinegar
½ (2-ounce) can anchovy fillets, drained and minced
3 tablespoons sliced green onion tops
3 tablespoons finely snipped parsley
  Romaine lettuce, torn in pieces
2 (7½-ounce) cans crabmeat, drained
6 hard-cooked eggs, thinly sliced
1 medium cucumber, thinly sliced
  Lemon wedges
  Sour Cream Dressing Mix

Combine sour cream, mayonnaise, vinegar, anchovies, onion tops, and parsley; mix well and chill. Arrange romaine on 6 chilled salad plates. Arrange crabmeat, eggs, and cucumber on romaine. Garnish with lemon wedges. Prepare Sour Cream Dressing Mix according to package directions. Serve with salad. Yield: 6 servings.

CRAB ASPARAGUS SALAD

1 pound crabmeat, fresh or frozen
    or
2 (6½-ounce) cans crabmeat
1 tablespoon freshly squeezed lemon juice
1 teaspoon salt
  Dash pepper
1 (14½-ounce) can asparagus spears
⅓ cup commercial French dressing
6 lettuce leaves
  Pimiento strips

Thaw frozen crabmeat or drain canned crabmeat. Remove any shell or cartilage from crabmeat. Sprinkle with lemon juice, salt, and pepper; mix lightly. Chill. Drain asparagus and place in a shallow baking dish. Pour French dressing over asparagus and let stand in refrigerator for at least 1 hour. Drain asparagus and place 3 spears on each lettuce leaf. Top each serving of asparagus with approximately ⅓ cup crabmeat. Garnish with pimiento strips. Serve with additional French dressing. Yield: 6 servings.

HOT CRAB SALAD

2 tablespoons minced onion
2 tablespoons minced green pepper
⅓ cup butter or margarine
2 cups cooked noodles
1½ cups milk
1 cup soft bread crumbs
1 cup shredded cheese
3 eggs, beaten
1 teaspoon salt
1½ cups crabmeat
  White Sauce

Sauté onion and green pepper in butter. Combine remaining ingredients except crabmeat; put in bottom of a greased 1½-quart baking dish. Top with crabmeat. Cover with White Sauce; bake at 350° for 1 hour. Yield: 10 servings.

White Sauce

1 tablespoon butter or margarine
2 tablespoons all-purpose flour
1½ cups milk
1 teaspoon salt
½ cup mayonnaise

Melt butter; blend in flour. Slowly stir in milk and salt. Cook until slightly thickened. Cool slightly; add mayonnaise, and pour over Hot Crab Salad.

CRAB SALAD IN LIME MOLD

1 pound crabmeat, fresh or frozen
　　　　or
2 (6½-ounce) cans crabmeat
1 (20-ounce) can pineapple tidbits
½ cup chopped pecans
½ cup mayonnaise or salad dressing
1 teaspoon freshly squeezed lemon juice
¼ teaspoon salt
　　Lime Mold
　　Salad greens

Thaw frozen crabmeat or drain canned crabmeat. Remove any shell or cartilage from crabmeat. Drain pineapple, reserving juice. Combine pineapple, pecans, mayonnaise, lemon juice, salt, and crabmeat; toss lightly. Chill. Unmold gelatin on salad greens; fill center with crab salad. Yield: 6 servings.

Lime Mold

2 (3-ounce) packages lime-flavored gelatin
1 teaspoon salt
1½ cups boiling water
1 cup canned pineapple juice
1 cup water
¼ cup freshly squeezed lemon juice

Dissolve gelatin and salt in boiling water. Add pineapple juice, water, and lemon juice; mix well. Pour into a 1-quart ring mold; chill until firm. Yield: 6 servings.

BARBECUED CRAB SANDWICHES

½ pound crabmeat
¼ cup chopped onion
½ cup chopped celery
3 tablespoons butter or margarine
¼ teaspoon salt
　　Dash pepper
2 whole bay leaves
2 whole cloves
2 teaspoons soy sauce
2 teaspoons Worcestershire sauce
1 chicken bouillon cube
½ cup tomato juice
2 tablespoons chopped parsley
6 large buttered rolls

Remove any shell or cartilage from crabmeat. Cook onion and celery in butter until tender. Add seasonings, bouillon cube, and tomato juice. Simmer for 5 minutes. Remove bay leaves and cloves. Add parsley and crabmeat; heat. Serve on rolls. Yield: 6 servings.

PEAS AND CRABMEAT SALAD

2 (6½-ounce) cans crabmeat
2 cups frozen peas, thawed
2 cups cooked rice
1 cup diced celery
1 teaspoon salt
½ teaspoon curry powder
⅔ cup mayonnaise
　　Crisp salad greens

Separate crab pieces, removing all shell or cartilage. Add remaining ingredients, except salad greens; mix gently to combine. Refrigerate, covered, for 1 hour. Serve on salad greens. Yield: 8 servings.

CRAB OR SHRIMP PUFFS

2 (6½-ounce) cans crabmeat or shrimp
1 cup finely chopped celery
½ cup mayonnaise or salad dressing
2 tablespoons chopped onion
2 tablespoons chopped sweet pickle
　　Salt to taste
　　Puff Shells

Drain crabmeat or shrimp; remove all shell or cartilage. Combine all ingredients except puff shells. Mix thoroughly. Cut tops from puff shells. Fill each with approximately 2 teaspoonsful of salad. Yield: about 55 hors d'oeuvres.

Puff Shells

½ cup boiling water
¼ cup butter or margarine
　　Dash salt
½ cup all-purpose flour
2 eggs

Combine water, butter and salt in a saucepan; bring to a boil. Add flour all at one time and stir vigorously until mixture forms a ball and leaves the sides of the pan. Remove from heat.

Add eggs, one at a time, beating thoroughly after each addition. Continue beating until a stiff dough is formed. Drop by level teaspoonsful on a well-greased 15- x 10- x 1-inch pan. Bake at 450° for 10 minutes. Reduce heat to 350° and continue baking about 10 minutes longer.
Yield: about 55 puff shells.

SOFT-SHELL CRABS, PECAN MONTELEONE

 4 **soft-shell crabs, cut in quarters**
   All-purpose flour
   Salt and pepper
 6 **tablespoons butter or margarine**
 1 **tablespoon finely chopped green onion**
 1 **tablespoon finely chopped parsley**
½ **cup absinthe liqueur**
 3 **egg yolks**
½ **cup cream**
   Salt and pepper
16 **tomato slices**
16 **toasted bread rounds**
½ **cup chopped pecans**
   Dash cayenne pepper

Clean soft-shell crabs, dry wth paper towel, and cut each crab into 4 parts. Toss crabs very lightly in flour seasoned with salt and pepper. Melt butter in heavy skillet; when hot, put in crabs, shell side down. Reduce heat and sauté crabs until brown. Turn crabs and brown on other side. When brown all over, remove to hot platter and keep warm.

Add 1 tablespoon of finely chopped onion and parsley to butter remaining in the skillet. Add ½ cup absinthe and simmer for 5 minutes. Have ready the yolks of 3 eggs beaten together with ½ cup cream. Add this to absinthe broth, being careful not to let the broth boil after the egg mixture has been added. Salt and pepper to taste.

To serve, place tomato slice on toasted bread round, top with a soft-shell crab quarter, spoon over absinthe sauce, and sprinkle with chopped pecans and cayenne pepper.
Yield: 16 hors d'oeuvres.

CRABMEAT SOUFFLE

 2 **tablespoons butter or margarine**
 2 **tablespoons all-purpose flour**
¾ **teaspoon salt**
⅛ **teaspoon pepper**
 1 **cup evaporated milk**
 1 **cup water**
½ **cup soft bread crumbs**
 2 **cups flaked cooked crabmeat**
 3 **egg yolks, well beaten**
 2 **teaspoons minced parsley**
 3 **egg whites, stiffly beaten**

Heat butter in skillet; add flour, salt, and pepper, and mix well. Add milk and water gradually and bring to boiling point, stirring constantly. Add breadcrumbs and cook 2 minutes

longer. Remove from heat; add crabmeat, egg yolks, and parsley. Fold in stiffly beaten egg whites. Put into a greased 2-quart baking dish and bake, uncovered, at 350° for about 50 minutes. Yield: 6 servings.

SPAGHETTI WITH CRAB SAUCE

 1 **pound crabmeat**
½ **cup chopped onion**
½ **cup chopped celery**
 2 **cloves garlic, finely chopped**
 2 **tablespoons chopped parsley**
¼ **cup butter or margarine, melted**
 1 **cup cooked tomatoes**
 1 **(8-ounce) can tomato sauce**
¼ **teaspoon salt**
½ **teaspoon paprika**
   Dash pepper
 3 **cups cooked spaghetti**
   Grated Parmesan cheese

Remove any shell or cartilage from crabmeat. Cook onion, celery, garlic, and parsley in butter until tender. Add tomatoes, tomato sauce, and seasonings. Simmer for 20 minutes, stirring occasionally. Add crabmeat; heat. Serve over spaghetti. Garnish with cheese sprinkled over the top. Yield: 6 servings.

NEW ORLEANS CRAB SPREAD

 2 **(6½-ounce) cans crabmeat**
¼ **cup tarragon vinegar**
⅓ **cup mayonnaise or salad dressing**
 3 **tablespoons chopped pimiento**
 2 **tablespoons chopped green onion**
 1 **teaspoon salt**
½ **teaspoon pepper**
 1 **tablespoon drained capers**
   Assorted chips, crackers, or raw vegetables

Drain crabmeat; remove any remaining shell or cartilage. Flake the crabmeat. Pour vinegar over crabmeat and chill for 30 minutes. Drain. Add mayonnaise, pimiento, onion, salt, and pepper; mix thoroughly. Garnish with capers. Serve with chips, crackers, or vegetables. Yield: about 2 cups.

MARYLAND STEAMED HARD-SHELL CRABS

Steamed hard-shell crabs may be prepared quickly and served hot or cold. (Although a few of your more squeamish guests may be reluctant to dine on something that must be cleaned while it is being eaten, resistance usually melts after the first taste of crabmeat.)

You will need a large pot (either a regular crab pot with rack, or a canner. For large feasts, use a clean garbage can). Purchase or catch your live blue channel crabs, and allow at least 3 to 4 crabs per person, more for experienced crab aficionados. To keep crabs inactive so they may be handled, keep them in a cooler.

Vinegar
Water
Seafood seasoning
Flake or table salt
Coarse ground black pepper
Cayenne pepper (optional)

Pour equal amounts of vinegar and water into the pot until the mixture is about an inch deep. Place your rack in the bottom of the pot to keep the crabs out of the liquid. If you don't have a rack, use clean rocks.

Place a single layer of crabs on the rack and sprinkle generously with a mixture of seafood seasoning, salt, pepper, and cayenne. Cover the pot; then steam until the crabs are red. This usually takes about 30 to 45 minutes, sometimes less. Try not to overcook, since overdone crabmeat is mushy rather than firm and flaky.

While crabs are steaming, cover the table with newspapers, and give each guest a dull table knife (wooden mallets are traditional, but table knives work just as well). Heap the finished crabs in the center of the table and let each guest fend for himself.

To eat hard-shells, break off the claws; then crack them open with the knife or mallet and dig out the meat. Then turn the body of the crab on its back and pull off the tab (on males — which are preferred — the tab is slender and white; on females, the tab is much wider and often darkly colored. In some states, female crabs are protected by law).

Place the edge of the knife in the groove you find under the tab, and hit the back of the blade with the heel of your hand to break the belly shell. Then, from each side, pull the belly shell and attached lumps of meat and legs. Discard the top shell. This gives you two large pieces of backfin

lump. Scrape any gills — often called "dead man" — that remain from each lump; then hold the legs and pull the paper-thin shell away from the meat.

Eat the meat with your fingers. As you eat, your fingers will pick up the hot seasoning from the outside of the shell, thus seasoning the meat as you handle it. Have a large glass of something cold and wet nearby. You'll need it.

CRAB STEW

2 to 2½ cups large, fresh, canned or thawed frozen King crabmeat, in chunks, completely drained
¼ cup butter or margarine
3 tablespoons minced onion
1½ teaspoons salt
⅛ teaspoon pepper
¼ teaspoon dried rosemary
2½ cups milk
1 cup heavy cream
2 tablespoons sherry
Chopped parsley

Remove cartilage from crabmeat, if canned. Melt butter in top of a double-boiler over direct heat. Add onion, and cook until tender. Add crabmeat, salt, pepper, and rosemary; cook over low heat, stirring occasionally, for 10 minutes. Set double-boiler top over boiling water; add milk, and cook 15 minutes. Add heavy cream. When hot, stir in sherry. Then sprinkle with parsley, and serve. Yield: 4 to 6 servings.

SOUTHERN CRAB STEW

4 dozen crabs
1 pound salt pork, cut into cubes
2 pounds onions
½ cup vinegar
Salt and pepper to taste
Catsup, Worcestershire sauce, and hot pepper sauce to taste
Cornmeal

Cook crabs; remove meat and set aside. Fry salt pork until brown and put in a deep pot. Add alternating layers of crabs and onions, peeled and sliced. Cover with hot water. Add vinegar and salt and pepper to taste. Bring to a boil and let boil for 15 minutes.

Add catsup, Worcestershire, and hot pepper sauce to taste. Cook 15 minutes longer. Sprinkle in a little cornmeal. Let cook until thickened. If not as thick as desired, add more cornmeal. Yield: 8 servings.

LOBSTER

The lobster is known as the "king of the shellfish," so take great care to treat him royally when he becomes your dinner. Frozen or canned lobster is available, but fresh is an ultimate taste treat.

To prepare a fresh lobster, remove and discard the black intestinal vein and the small stomach sac. Also, throw away the grayish, fringy-looking portions of the upper body.

If you intend to broil the lobster, make certain that you clean it before it is cooked. If it is to be boiled, clean it after cooking. Boiling is considered to be the best way to prepare the lobster. To boil, plunge the lobster headfirst into boiling, salted water. For those who like their lobster hot, cook for 20 to 25 minutes; serve with melted butter and lemon wedges. For cold lobster lovers, cook for 15 minutes, let stand in the cooking liquid until cooled, and eat cold or combine in a casserole.

LOBSTER AMANDINE

- 1 pound cooked lobster meat
- 1 cup blanched, slivered almonds
- ½ cup butter or margarine, melted
- ½ teaspoon salt
  Dash pepper
- 2 tablespoons chopped parsley
  Toast points

Cut lobster meat into 1-inch pieces. Sauté almonds in butter until lightly brown. Remove almonds. Add lobster meat and sauté until lightly browned. Add seasonings, parsley, and almonds. Serve on toast points. Yield: 6 servings.

LOBSTER ANDALOUSE

- 4 frozen lobster tails
- 5 tablespoons butter or margarine
- 1 clove fresh garlic, crushed
  Juice of 1 lemon
- 1 cup finely chopped parsley
- 1½ cups vermouth
  Lemon slices and parsley

Cut lobster in 1-inch chunks. Put butter in skillet, add crushed garlic, and cook at low heat until butter is well seasoned. Remove garlic. Add lobster to garlic butter and stir until cooked (from 10 to 15 minutes). Add lemon juice and parsley and cook about 3 minutes longer. Add vermouth and set aflame. When flame dies down, serve at once. Garnish with lemon slices and parsley. Yield: 4 servings.

SHERRIED LOBSTER BISQUE

- 2 (10¾-ounce) cans cream of mushroom soup, undiluted
- 2 (10¾-ounce) cans tomato soup, undiluted
- ⅔ cup dry sherry
- 1 cup half-and-half
- 2½ cups milk
- 1 (5-ounce) can lobster meat
  Sliced green onion

Combine cream of mushroom soup and tomato soup in a large saucepan; mix well. Stir in sherry, half-and-half, and milk. Drain lobster meat; remove membrane. Add lobster to soup. Bring just to boiling over medium heat, stirring occasionally. To serve: Pour soup into a warm tureen or soup cups. Garnish with sliced green onion. Yield: 10 servings.

BAKED STUFFED LOBSTERS

2 live lobsters (1 pound each)
2 cups soft bread cubes
2 tablespoons butter or margarine, melted
1 tablespoon grated onion
   Dash garlic salt

Place live lobster on its back; insert a sharp knife between body shell and tail segment, cutting down to sever the spinal cord. Cut in half lengthwise. Remove the stomach, which is just back of the head, and the intestinal vein, which runs from the stomach to the tip of the tail. Remove and save the green liver and coral roe. Crack claws. Repeat with second lobster.

Combine bread cubes, butter, onion, garlic salt, green liver, and coral roe. Place in body cavity and spread over surface of tail meat. Place in a 15½ - x 10½ - x 1-inch baking dish. Bake at 400° for 20 to 25 minutes or until lightly browned. Yield: 2 servings.

LOBSTER GUNDY

2 cups cooked lobster meat
½ cup finely chopped onion
4 ounces pimiento, drained and chopped
¼ cup salad oil
2 tablespoons freshly squeezed lime juice
½ teaspoon salt
   Few drops hot pepper sauce
   Lettuce leaves
   Parsley sprigs, cooked carrots, and beets
   for garnish

Put lobster through grinder. Add next 6 ingredients and mix well. Chill. Place on lettuce leaves and garnish the mound with sprigs of parsley, cooked carrots, and beets. Yield: 6 servings.

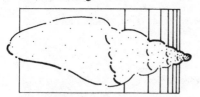

BROILED LOBSTERS

2 live lobsters (1 pound each)
1 tablespoon butter or margarine, melted
¼ teaspoon salt
   Dash white pepper
   Dash paprika
¼ cup butter or margarine, melted
1 tablespoon freshly squeezed lemon juice

Place live lobster on its back; insert a sharp knife between body shell and tail segment, cutting down to sever the spinal cord. Cut in half lengthwise. Remove the stomach, which is just back of the head, and the intestinal vein, which runs from the stomach to the tip of the tail. Do not discard the green liver and coral roe; they are delicious. Crack claws. Repeat with second lobster. Lay lobsters open as flat as possible on a broiler pan. Brush lobster meat with butter. Sprinkle with salt, pepper, and paprika. Broil about 4 inches from source of heat for 12 to 15 minutes or until lightly browned. Combine butter and lemon juice; serve with lobsters. Yield: 2 servings.

BROILED BOILED LOBSTERS

2 boiled lobsters
1 tablespoon butter or margarine, melted
   Dash white pepper
   Dash paprika
¼ cup butter or margarine, melted
1 tablespoon freshly squeezed lemon juice

Lay lobsters open as flat as possible on a broiler pan. Brush lobster meat with butter. Sprinkle with pepper and paprika. Broil about 4 inches from source of heat for 5 minutes or until lightly browned. Combine butter and lemon juice; serve with lobsters. Yield: 2 servings.

BROILED LOBSTER TAILS

Thaw tails if frozen. Cut under-shell along edges and remove. Insert skewer close to shell at tail end. Broil shell side up 5 inches below the unit. Turn flesh side up, spread with butter or margarine, and broil just until flesh is tender. Overcooking toughens lobster. See chart for timing. Serve in shell with melted butter and lemon wedges. Allow ½ pound per person.

Time Chart for Broiling Lobster

Weight	4-6 oz.	7-9 oz.	10-12 oz.	13-16 oz.
Shell Side	5 min.	5 min.	5 min.	5 min.
Flesh Side	6 min.	7 min.	8 min.	9 min.

If no skewers are available to keep tail flat, bend tail backwards toward shell side to crack. This prevents curling.

Grapefruit halves, seasoned with a dash of crème de menthe, may be broiled along with the lobster.

LOBSTER MOUSSE

½ pound cooked lobster meat
 1 tablespoon unflavored gelatin
¼ cup cold water
½ cup boiling water
½ cup chopped celery
 2 tablespoons sliced stuffed olives
 1 tablespoon grated onion
 1 teaspoon prepared mustard
½ teaspoon salt
½ cup whipping cream
¼ cup mayonnaise or salad dressing
    Salad greens

Cut lobster meat into ½-inch pieces. Soften gelatin in cold water for 5 minutes. Add boiling water and stir until dissolved. Add the next 5 ingredients. Chill until almost congealed. Add lobster meat. Whip cream. Combine mayonnaise and whipped cream; fold into gelatin mixture. Place in a 1-quart mold; chill until firm. Unmold on salad greens. Yield: 6 servings.

FROZEN LOBSTER SALAD

½ pound cooked lobster meat
 1 (3-ounce) package cream cheese
½ cup mayonnaise or salad dressing
 2 tablespoons chopped pimiento
½ cup chopped nuts
½ teaspoon salt
 5 drops hot pepper sauce
½ cup whipping cream
    Lettuce

Cut lobster meat into ½-inch pieces. Cream cheese and mayonnaise. Add the next four ingredients and lobster meat. Whip cream. Fold in whipped cream. Place in a 1-quart ice cube tray; freeze. Remove from freezer and let stand at room temperature for 15 minutes before serving. Cut into 6 slices and serve on lettuce. Yield: 6 servings.

SPECIAL LOBSTER NEWBURG

 3 tablespoons salad oil
 3 tablespoons cornstarch
½ teaspoon salt
1½ cups milk
 2 cups bite-size pieces cooked lobster
 1 cup sliced celery
 2 tablespoons chili sauce
 2 teaspoons freshly squeezed lemon juice
    Dash paprika
    Cooked rice
    Parsley sprigs or olive slices

Heat salad oil in a saucepan. Blend in cornstarch and salt. Remove from heat. Gradually add milk, stirring until mixture is smooth. Cook over medium heat, stirring constantly, until mixture comes to a boil. Reduce heat and simmer for 1 minute. Add lobster, celery, chili sauce, lemon juice, and paprika. Heat. Serve over rice. Garnish with sprigs of parsley or olive slices. Yield: 4 servings.

LOBSTER NEWBURG

¼ cup butter or margarine
 2 tablespoons all-purpose flour
¼ teaspoon salt
¼ teaspoon ground nutmeg
½ teaspoon paprika
 1 cup heavy cream
 3 egg yolks, slightly beaten
 2 cups coarsely chopped, boiled lobster
 2 tablespoons sherry
 3 cups cooked rice

Melt butter in top of double boiler, over direct heat; remove from heat. Stir in flour to make a smooth paste. Add salt, nutmeg, and paprika. Gradually stir in cream. Bring to a boil, stirring constantly; reduce heat, and simmer, stirring, 3 minutes longer. Stir a little of hot mixture into egg yolks; pour back into top of double boiler. Add lobster and put over hot water; cook, stirring constantly, until mixture is thickened and lobster is hot, about 10 minutes. (Do not boil.)
Stir in sherry. Serve over hot rice. Yield: 4 servings.

LOBSTER-STUFFED EGGS

 1 pound cooked lobster meat
⅔ cup mayonnaise or salad dressing
 1 tablespoon chili sauce
 1 teaspoon grated onion
 1 teaspoon chopped green pepper
 1 teaspoon chopped pimiento
1½ dozen hard-cooked eggs
    Parsley

Chop lobster meat. Add mayonnaise, chili sauce, onion, green pepper, and pimiento. Chill. Cut eggs in half lengthwise and remove yolks. Mash yolks, add to lobster mixture, and place in egg whites. Garnish with parsley. Yield: 36 canapés.

SEAFOOD-AVOCADO SALAD
WITH DRESSING

 1 (6½-ounce) can lobster meat (about 1 cup)
 2 (6-ounce) packages quick-frozen crabmeat
   (about 2 cups)
 2 cups cooked shrimp, fresh, quick-frozen,
   or canned
   French dressing
 3 ripe avocados
 ½ cup mayonnaise
 ½ cup commercial sour cream
 1 tablespoon cut chives
   Cucumber and tomato slices

Remove any bits of shell from lobster and crabmeat and break into bite-size pieces. Reserve claw meat of lobster and a few whole shrimp for garnish. Cut remaining shrimp in pieces. Combine lobster, crabmeat, and shrimp. Add just enough French dressing to coat generously and chill. Just before serving, halve avocados, remove pit, and fill with seafood mixture. Combine mayonnaise, sour cream, and chives for dressing and top each avocado with a generous spoonful. Garnish with lobster claw meat and whole shrimp. Arrange on platter or chop plate and surround with overlapping alternate slices of cucumber and tomato. Yield: 6 servings.

LOBSTER STEW

 ¾ pound cooked lobster meat
 1 teaspoon salt
 ¼ teaspoon paprika
   Dash white pepper
   Dash ground nutmeg
 ¼ cup butter or margarine, melted
 1 pint milk
 1 pint half-and-half
   Chopped parsley

Cut lobster meat into ½-inch pieces. Add seasonings and lobster meat to butter; heat. Add milk and half-and-half and bring almost to boiling point. Garnish with parsley sprinkled over the top. Yield: 6 servings.

LOBSTER WAFFLES

 ½ pound cooked lobster meat
 3 cups commercial waffle mix
   Lemon Butter or Cheese Sauce

Chop lobster meat. Prepare waffle mix as directed. Add lobster meat. Bake in a hot waffle iron until brown. Serve with Lemon Butter or Cheese Sauce. Yield: 6 (7-inch) waffles.

Lemon Butter

 ½ cup butter or margarine
 1 teaspoon freshly squeezed lemon juice
 ¼ teaspoon grated lemon rind

Whip butter. Slowly add lemon juice and rind.

Cheese Sauce

 1 (10¾-ounce) can cheese soup
 ⅓ cup milk

Combine cheese soup and milk. Heat.

BROILED SPINY LOBSTER TAILS

 6 frozen spiny lobster tails (5 to 8 ounces each)
 ⅓ cup butter or margarine, melted
 ½ teaspoon salt
   Dash white pepper
   Dash paprika
 ¾ cup butter or margarine, melted
 3 tablespoons freshly squeezed lemon juice

Thaw lobster tails. Cut in half lengthwise. Lay lobster tails open as flat as possible on a broiler pan. Brush lobster meat with butter. Sprinkle with salt, pepper, and paprika. Broil about 4 inches from source of heat for 10 to 15 minutes, depending on size of lobster tails. Combine butter and lemon juice; serve with lobster tails. Yield: 6 servings.

LOBSTER THERMIDOR

 3 boiled lobsters
 2 tablespoons butter or margarine
 2 tablespoons all-purpose flour
 ½ teaspoon salt
 1½ teaspoons dry mustard
   Dash cayenne pepper
 1 cup half-and-half
 1 (4-ounce) can mushroom stems and pieces,
   drained
   Grated Parmesan cheese
   Paprika

Split lobsters lengthwise and remove meat. Clean shells and rinse. Cut lobster meat into ½-inch pieces. Melt butter; blend in flour and seasonings. Add half-and-half gradually and cook until thick and smooth, stirring constantly. Add mushrooms and lobster meat. Place in shells. Sprinkle with cheese and paprika. Place on a cookie sheet and bake at 400° for 10 minutes, or until brown. Yield: 6 servings.

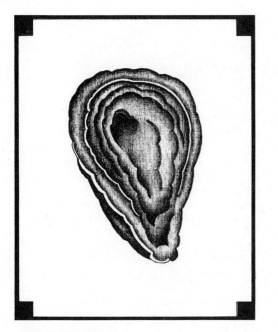

OYSTERS

Although there is a popular belief that oysters should only be eaten in months with names that contain an "r", this is not entirely true. Due to advanced methods of food preservation, they are available (and delicious) year-round.

Oysters may be bought in the shell, fresh or frozen, shucked, or canned. Oysters in the shell are generally sold by the dozen. The shells of the oyster should be tightly closed, indicating that the oysters are alive. Gaping shells that do not close when handled are evidence that the oysters within are dead and therefore not safe for use. Shell oysters should be kept refrigerated at about 40° for no longer than 20 days.

Shucked oysters are oysters which have been removed from the shell and which are generally sold by the pint or quart. These should be plump, creamy-colored with a clear liquid, and free from shell particles. The containers of the shucked oysters should be refrigerated or surrounded by ice. When properly handled, they will remain fresh for a week to 10 days.

The amount of oysters to be purchased depends on their use. For 6 people, allow at least 3 dozen shell oysters, 1 quart of shucked oysters, or 2 (7½-ounce) cans.

OYSTER BEIGNETS

1 (7½- or 8-ounce) can oysters
1 cup all-purpose flour
½ teaspoon sugar
¼ cup butter or margarine
1 cup milk
4 eggs
  Cocktail Sauce

Drain oysters well. Chop. Combine flour and sugar and sift. Combine butter and milk in a saucepan; place on low heat. Add flour all at one time and stir vigorously until mixture forms a ball and leaves the sides of the pan. Remove from heat. Add unbeaten eggs, one at a time, beating thoroughly after each addition; continue beating until a stiff batter is formed. Add oysters to the batter and mix well. Drop the mixture by teaspoonsful into deep fat, 350°. Fry approximately 5 to 6 minutes, or until brown. Drain on absorbent paper. Serve with cocktail sauce. Yield: approximately 60 beignets.

Cocktail Sauce

¾ cup chili sauce
¼ cup finely chopped celery
1 tablespoon freshly squeezed lemon juice
1 tablespoon horseradish
½ teaspoon salt

Combine all ingredients and chill.
Yield: 1 cup.

CASSEROLE OF OYSTERS AND MACARONI

2 dozen shucked oysters
3 cups shell macaroni
1 teaspoon salt
¼ teaspoon pepper
½ teaspoon paprika
2 cups (½ pound) shredded sharp Cheddar cheese
6 tablespoons melted butter or margarine
1 cup soft bread crumbs

Drain oysters, reserving ½ cup liquid. Cook macaroni, according to package directions, until barely tender; drain; rinse. In a 12- x 8- x 2-inch baking dish, arrange one third of macaroni, then half of oysters. Sprinkle with half of salt, pepper, and paprika; one third of cheese; then 2 tablespoons butter. Repeat. Spread rest of macaroni on top. Pour on reserved oyster liquid. Top with remaining butter tossed with crumbs; then sprinkle on rest of cheese. Refrigerate. Bake at 400° for 30 minutes, or until hot and lightly browned. Yield: 8 servings.

CREOLE OYSTER PIE

1 cup all-purpose flour
¼ teaspoon salt
⅓ cup vegetable shortening
1 tablespoon cold water
1 quart oysters, drained
1 cup all-purpose flour
2 teaspoons salt, divided
¼ teaspoon pepper
⅛ teaspoon ground mace
¼ teaspoon paprika
2 slices bacon, diced
1 small onion, minced
1 tablespoon minced green pepper
8 to 10 drops hot pepper sauce
   Juice of 1 large lemon (about 2 tablespoons)
1 tablespoon minced parsley, fresh, frozen,
   or dried
2 tablespoons butter

In a large bowl blend 1 cup flour, ¼ teaspoon salt, shortening, and water. Roll to ¼-inch thickness on lightly floured board. Cut into six rounds, 2¾ inches in diameter, using a regular-size glass as a cutter. Then remove center of each round with 1-inch biscuit cutter. Set aside pastry rounds while preparing rest of recipe.

Dry the drained oysters on paper towels. Roll in mixture of 1 cup flour, 1 teaspoon salt, ¼ teaspoon pepper, ⅛ teaspoon mace, and ¼ teaspoon paprika. Sauté bacon and onion until crisp and brown.

Place a layer of oysters close together in a buttered 10½- x 6½- x 2-inch baking dish. Sprinkle half of bacon and onion mixture over oysters. Add half of minced green pepper, hot pepper sauce, 1 teaspoon salt, lemon juice, and parsley. Repeat layers. Dot with butter and place all the pastry rounds on top. Bake at 450° for 25 minutes, or until pastry rounds are golden. Serve at once. Yield: 6 servings.

TASTY BAKED OYSTERS

36 shell oysters
 2 tablespoons minced onion
½ teaspoon salt
¼ teaspoon pepper
¼ teaspoon marjoram (optional)
   Butter

Shuck and drain oysters; place on deep half of shells. Sprinkle with onion, salt, pepper, and marjoram. Dot with butter. Place oysters in baking pan, and bake at 400° for 10 minutes, or until edges curl. Yield: 6 servings.

OYSTERS AU GRATIN

1 pint oysters
6 slices buttered toast
2 eggs, beaten
1 teaspoon salt
1 teaspoon prepared mustard
½ teaspoon paprika
½ cup milk
1 cup shredded American cheese

Drain oysters and set aside. Trim crusts from bread. Cut each slice into quarters. Combine beaten eggs, seasonings, and milk. Arrange layer of bread in a buttered casserole dish; cover with layer of oysters. Sprinkle with shredded cheese. Repeat layer, pour milk mixture over contents of dish, and cover with grated cheese. Place casserole in pan of hot water, bake at 350° for 30 minutes, or until brown. Yield: 6 servings.

OYSTER AND MACARONI CASSEROLE

1 pint oysters
1 (8-ounce) package elbow macaroni, cooked
   Cream
   Salt and pepper
¾ cup bread crumbs, packed

Drain oysters. In a 1½-quart casserole dish, place layers of oysters, then cooked macaroni; add cream, salt and pepper and cover with bread crumbs. Cover casserole and bake at 350° for about 1 hour. Take cover off casserole the last 15 minutes of baking time to brown crumbs. Yield: 6 to 7 servings.

ANGELS ON HORSEBACK

 1 pint select oysters
12 slices bacon, cut in half
½ teaspoon salt
⅛ teaspoon pepper
⅛ teaspoon paprika
 2 tablespoons chopped parsley

Drain oysters and place each oyster across half a slice of bacon. Sprinkle with seasonings and chopped parsley. Roll bacon around oyster and fasten with a toothpick. Place oysters on a rack in a shallow baking pan and bake at 450° for about 10 minutes, or until bacon is crisp. Remove toothpicks and serve. Yield: 6 servings.

OYSTERS CASINO

3 slices bacon
4 tablespoons chopped onion
2 tablespoons chopped green pepper
2 tablespoons chopped celery
1 teaspoon freshly squeezed lemon juice
½ teaspoon salt
Dash pepper
½ teaspoon Worcestershire sauce
2 drops hot pepper sauce
1 pint oysters, drained

Fry bacon and crumble. Add onion, green pepper, and celery and cook in bacon drippings until tender. Add lemon juice, salt, pepper, Worcestershire sauce, and hot pepper sauce and mix well. Arrange drained oysters in a buttered baking dish. Spread bacon mixture over oysters. Bake at 350° for about 10 minutes or until brown. Yield: 6 servings.

BROILED OYSTERS ON THE HALF SHELL

36 shell oysters
½ teaspoon salt
⅛ teaspoon pepper
½ cup bread crumbs
2 tablespoons butter or margarine, melted

Shuck and drain oysters; place on deep half of shell. Toss bread crumbs with melted butter. Sprinkle with salt, pepper, and buttered bread crumbs. Place on preheated broiler pan about 3 inches from source of heat, and broil for 5 minutes or until brown. Yield: 6 servings.

OYSTERS AND MACARONI AU GRATIN

1 pint oysters
3 tablespoons butter or margarine
3 tablespoons all-purpose flour
1½ cups milk
1 cup cooked macaroni
1 teaspoon salt
⅛ teaspoon pepper
1 cup shredded American cheese

Drain oysters. Melt butter in top of double boiler, blend in flour, add milk, and cook until thick, stirring constantly. Place layer of macaroni in a buttered casserole dish; cover with layer of oysters; sprinkle with salt, pepper, and cheese. Repeat layer, pour sauce over contents of dish and cover with cheese. Bake at 350° for 30 minutes, or until brown. Yield: 6 servings.

OYSTER CHOWDER

3 tablespoons chopped onion
3 tablespoons butter or margarine
1 cup water
⅔ cup diced celery
2 cups diced potatoes
1 tablespoon salt
½ teaspoon pepper
4 cups milk
1 pint oysters, including liquor
Chopped parsley

Sauté onion in butter until slightly brown; add water, celery, potatoes, salt, and pepper. Cover and cook until vegetables are tender. Add milk and let come to boiling point. Simmer oysters in their liquor for about 5 minutes or until edges curl. Drain. Combine with milk and vegetables. Serve immediately with chopped parsley sprinkled over the top. Yield: 6 servings.

OYSTERS CREOLE

1 pint oysters
3 tablespoons chopped onion
2 tablespoons butter or margarine
3 tablespoons all-purpose flour
1 cup tomato juice
2 tablespoons chopped parsley
¼ teaspoon hot pepper sauce
¾ teaspoon salt
Buttered toast

Drain oysters. Cook onion in butter until tender. Blend in flour; add tomato juice and cook until thick, stirring constantly. Add oysters, seasonings, and simmer for about 5 minutes, or until edges begin to curl. Serve on toast. Yield: 6 servings.

BROILED OYSTERS

Crumbled crackers
8 to 10 crab shells
1 quart oysters
2 tablespoons butter
1 whole lemon, cut into pieces
1 tablespoon Worcestershire sauce
½ teaspoon pepper
2 tablespoons hot water

Put crumbled crackers in crab shells to cover bottom of shells. Place oysters over the crumbled crackers. Heat together the other ingredients, and put 1 teaspoon mixture over each shell of oysters. Place oysters under the broiler and broil about 5 minutes. Yield: 8 to 10 servings.

SOUTHERN OYSTER CHOWDER

- 3 tablespoons chopped onion
- 3 tablespoons butter or margarine
- 1 cup water
- ¼ cup diced celery
- 4 cups diced potatoes
- 2½ teaspoons salt
- ¼ teaspoon pepper
- 1 cup evaporated milk
- 3 cups water
- 1½ pints small oysters

Sauté onion in butter. Add water, celery, and potatoes. Cover and cook until nearly done. Season with salt and pepper. When the vegetables are tender, add the milk and let come to a boil. Remove from heat. Add 3 cups water to oysters and heat, removing any scum that accumulates on surface. When edges curl, combine with milk and vegetables. Let stand a few minutes for flavors to blend. Serve hot. Yield: 6 servings.

DEVILED OYSTERS AND TURKEY IN TOAST CUPS

- ¾ cup butter or margarine
- ¾ cup all-purpose flour
  Dash pepper
- 2 (2¼-ounce) cans deviled ham
- 6 cups milk
- 2 dozen oysters (more if desired), including liquor
- 3 cups diced turkey
  Toast Cups

Melt butter; blend in flour, pepper, and deviled ham. Add milk and cook over low heat, stirring until mixture is smooth and thick. Add oysters, oyster liquor, and diced turkey. Heat thoroughly. Serve in Toast Cups. Yield: 12 servings.

Toast Cups

Remove crusts from thin slices of bread; press each slice in section of muffin pan. Spread generously with melted butter or margarine. Bake at 500° to brown.

SEA COAST DIABLE

- 1 (27-ounce) can spinach or other greens, drained
- ½ cup cream of celery soup
  Dash ground nutmeg
- 2 (8-ounce) cans oysters, drained
- 2 (4½- to 6½-ounce) cans shrimp, drained
- 1 clove garlic, minced
- ¼ cup butter or margarine
- ½ teaspoon Worcestershire sauce
  Dash hot pepper sauce
- 2 tablespoons grated Parmesan cheese

Combine drained spinach, soup, and nutmeg. Line a greased shallow 1½-quart baking dish with spinach mixture. Arrange drained oysters on spinach. Cover oysters with drained rinsed shrimp. Sauté minced garlic in butter; add Worcestershire sauce and hot pepper sauce. Drizzle butter mixture over oysters and shrimp. Cover and bake at 350° for 35 minutes, or until heated through. Remove cover; sprinkle with Parmesan cheese and place under broiler several minutes to brown the cheese. Yield: 6 servings.

FRIED OYSTERS

- 1 quart select oysters
- 2 eggs, beaten
- 2 tablespoons milk
- 1 teaspoon salt
  Dash pepper
- 1 cup bread crumbs, cracker crumbs, or cornmeal

Drain oysters. Combine eggs, milk, and seasonings. Dip oysters in egg mixture and roll in crumbs.

Panfried

Place oysters in a heavy frying pan which contains about ⅛ inch of shortening, hot but not smoking. Fry at moderate heat. When oysters are brown on one side, turn carefully and brown the other side. Cooking time is approximately 5 minutes. Drain on absorbent paper. Yield: 6 servings.

Deep Fat Fried

Fry in a basket in deep fat at 375° for 2 to 3 minutes, or until brown. Drain on absorbent paper. Yield: 6 servings.

ESCALLOPED OYSTERS

½ cup butter or margarine
½ cup all-purpose flour
½ teaspoon salt
¼ teaspoon pepper
½ teaspoon paprika
1 medium onion, minced
1 teaspoon freshly squeezed lemon juice
1 tablespoon Worcestershire sauce
1 quart oysters
¼ cup cracker crumbs

Melt butter; add flour and cook for 5 minutes, or until light brown. Add salt, pepper, paprika; cook for 3 minutes. Add minced onion and green pepper. Cook slowly for 5 minutes. Remove from heat; add lemon juice, Worcestershire sauce, and oysters which have been heated in their own liquid. Pour in baking dish and sprinkle with crumbs. Bake at 400° for 30 minutes. Yield: 8 to 10 servings.

OYSTER FRITTERS

1 pint oysters
2 cups all-purpose flour
1 tablespoon baking powder
1½ teaspoons salt
2 eggs, beaten
1 cup milk
1 tablespoon butter or margarine, melted
Shortening or salad oil for frying

Drain oysters, and chop. Combine dry ingredients. Combine beaten eggs, milk, and butter. Pour into dry ingredients and stir until smooth. Add oysters. Drop batter by teaspoonsful into hot shortening heated to 350° and fry for about 3 minutes, or until golden brown. Drain on absorbent paper. Yield: 6 servings.

OYSTER KABOBS

6 slices bacon
1 pint select oysters
4 tomatoes, sliced
½ teaspoon salt
Dash pepper

Cut bacon into 2-inch pieces. Arrange a piece of bacon, an oyster, and a thick slice of tomato on skewers, leaving a little space between each. Continue to repeat ingredients on skewer. Sprinkle with salt and pepper and place skewers across baking dish. Bake at 500° for about 20 minutes, or until bacon is crisp. Yield: 6 servings.

OYSTER JAMBALAYA

1 pint oysters
1 cup uncooked regular rice
3 tablespoons salad oil
½ cup minced onion
½ cup minced celery
1 small green pepper, minced
2 cloves garlic, minced
2 cups boiling water
½ cup reserved oyster liquor, heated
Salt and pepper to taste
Butter (optional)

Drain oysters and reserve liquor. Put rice into heated shortening in a heavy saucepan; stir until lightly browned. Add minced ingredients and sauté for about 1 minute. Add boiling water and oyster liquor, salt, and pepper, and mix thoroughly. Add oysters or other seafood, stir once, reduce heat to simmer, cover and cook for about 15 minutes, or until rice is tender. If desired, after rice is done, place about four pats of butter on top, cover, and allow to melt. Yield: 4 servings.

OYSTERS "JOHNNY REB"

2 quarts oysters, drained
½ cup finely chopped parsley
½ cup finely chopped shallots or onions
Salt and pepper to taste
Hot pepper sauce to taste
1 tablespoon Worcestershire sauce
2 tablespoons freshly squeezed lemon juice
½ cup melted butter or margarine
2 cups fine cracker crumbs
Paprika
¾ cup half-and-half

Place a layer of oysters in the bottom of a greased shallow 2-quart baking dish. Sprinkle with half of parsley, shallots, seasonings, lemon juice, butter, and crumbs. Make another layer of the same. Sprinkle with paprika. Just before baking, pour the half-and-half into evenly spaced holes, being very careful not to moisten crumb topping all over. Bake at 375° for about 30 minutes, or until firm. Yield: 12 to 15 servings.

OYSTERS ON THE HALF SHELL

36　shell oysters
　　Cocktail sauce
　　Lemon wedges

Shuck oysters. Arrange a bed of crushed ice in shallow bowls or soup plates. Place six half-shell oysters on the ice with small bowl of cocktail sauce in center. Garnish with lemon wedges. Yield: 6 servings.

Variation: Season oysters on half shell with salt and pepper. Sprinkle buttered crumbs on top. Dust with paprika and broil 3 inches from source of heat for 5 minutes.

OYSTERS ROCKEFELLER

36　shell oysters
　2　cups cooked spinach
　4　tablespoons chopped onion
　2　bay leaves
　1　tablespoon parsley
　½　teaspoon celery salt
　½　teaspoon salt
　6　drops hot pepper sauce
　6　tablespoons butter or margarine
　½　cup bread crumbs
　　Lemon slices

Shuck and drain oysters; place on deep half of shells. Put spinach, onion, bay leaves, and parsley through food grinder. Add seasonings to spinach, and cook in butter for 5 minutes. Add bread crumbs and mix well. Spread mixture over oysters, and bake at 400° for about 10 minutes. Garnish with lemon slices. Yield: 6 servings.

SCALLOPED OYSTERS

　2　(7½- or 8-ounce) cans oysters
　¾　cup dry bread crumbs
　¾　cup unsalted cracker crumbs
　　Dash pepper
　½　cup melted butter or margarine
　¼　teaspoon Worcestershire sauce
　1　cup milk

Drain oysters. Combine crumbs, pepper, and butter. Sprinkle one-third of the buttered, seasoned crumbs in a well-greased, round 8- x 8- x 2-inch baking dish. Cover with a layer of oysters; repeat layers. Add Worcestershire sauce to milk and pour over oysters. Sprinkle remaining crumbs over the top. Bake at 400° for 20 to 25 minutes or until brown. Yield: 6 servings.

OYSTER STEW

　4　tablespoons butter or margarine
　1　pint oysters, drained
　4　cups milk
1½　teaspoons salt
　⅛　teaspoon pepper
　　Paprika

Melt butter, add drained oysters, and cook for 3 minutes or until edges curl. Add milk, salt, and pepper, and bring almost to boiling point. Serve at once. Garnish with paprika. Yield: 6 servings.

OYSTER STUFFING

　1　pint oysters
　½　cup chopped celery
　½　cup chopped onion
　¼　cup salad oil, butter, or margarine, melted
　4　cups soft bread cubes
　1　tablespoon chopped parsley
　1　teaspoon salt
　　Dash poultry seasoning
　　Dash pepper

Drain oysters, saving liquor. Remove any pieces of shell. Chop oysters. Cook celery and onion in shortening until tender. Combine cooked vegetables, bread cubes, parsley, seasonings, and oysters. Mix thoroughly. If stuffing seems dry, moisten with oyster liquor. Yield: enough for a 4-pound bird.

Stuffing for Turkey

　For 5 - 9 pound Turkey
　　2 times above stuffing recipe
　For 10 -15 pound Turkey
　　3 times above stuffing recipe
　For 16 -20 pound Turkey
　　4 times above stuffing recipe
　For 21 - 25 pound Turkey
　　5 times above stuffing recipe

SALMON

Salmon is available fresh in some markets, but in our Southern stores, we rely primarily on the canned product. Salmon contains an excellent quality protein and furnishes other valuable nutrients such as vitamin A, thiamin, and niacin.

The color of the salmon flesh may vary from almost white to the characteristic bright red. The red and pink varieties are available in most supermarkets. Salmon may be prepared in a variety of ways, or it may be eaten directly from the can.

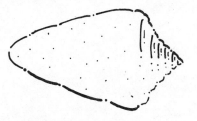

SALMON BALLS

- 1 (1-pound) can salmon
- 1 egg
- ¼ cup milk
- 1 teaspoon salt
- ⅛ teaspoon pepper
- ⅛ teaspoon celery salt
- ½ teaspoon Worcestershire sauce
- 1 cup soft bread crumbs
  Shortening or salad oil

Drain salmon; remove bones and flake very fine. Beat egg until light. Add milk, salt, pepper, celery salt, and Worcestershire sauce to egg; mix well. Mix salmon and bread crumbs together. Stir in the egg and milk mixture. Form mixture into eight (1½-inch) balls. Heat enough shortening to make a depth of 3 inches in a heavy skillet. Heat shortening to 365°. Drop balls into hot shortening and cook for 5 minutes or until brown. Yield: 8 servings.

SALMON BON MARCHE

- 1 (1-pound) can salmon
- ¼ cup chopped onion
- ¼ cup melted butter or margarine
- ¼ cup all-purpose flour
- ½ teaspoon salt
  Pepper to taste
- 2 cups milk
- 1 (8½-ounce) can peas and carrots, undrained
  Biscuits, cornbread, or toast

Drain liquid from salmon; reserve liquid. Break salmon into large pieces. Sauté onion in butter until wilted; stir in flour, salt, and pepper. Add milk a little at a time; stir constantly until mixture is thick. Add vegetables, salmon, and salmon liquid; heat. Serve over biscuits. Yield: 6 servings.

SALMON BURGERS

- 1 (1-pound) can salmon
- ½ cup chopped onion
- ¼ cup melted butter or margarine
- ⅓ cup dry bread crumbs
- 2 eggs, beaten
- 1 teaspoon prepared mustard
- ½ teaspoon salt
- ½ cup dry bread crumbs
  Shortening
- 6 buttered hamburger rolls

Drain liquid from salmon; reserve liquid. Break salmon into small pieces.

Sauté onion in butter until tender. Mix onion, ⅓ cup bread crumbs, eggs, mustard, salt, salmon, and salmon liquid. Make 6 salmon burgers. Roll salmon burgers in ½ cup bread crumbs and fry in hot shortening for 3 to 4 minutes on each side or until brown. Drain on paper towels. Serve on warm hamburger rolls. Yield: 6 servings.

DELICIOUS SALMON CASSEROLE

1 (5-ounce) package noodles
1 (1-pound) can salmon
1 (10¾-ounce) can cream of mushroom soup
1¼ cups milk
¼ cup chopped onion (optional)
¼ to ½ cup diced celery (optional)
1 teaspoon salt
⅛ teaspoon pepper
½ cup buttered bread crumbs
   Butter
   Paprika

Cook noodles in boiling salted water until tender. Drain in colander; rinse well with boiling water. Alternate layers of noodles and salmon in a 2-quart casserole dish. Combine soup, milk, onion and celery (if desired), salt, and pepper; pour over salmon and noodle mixture. Sprinkle bread crumbs over top; dot with butter and sprinkle with paprika. Bake at 350° for about 30 minutes. Serve hot. Yield: 6 to 8 servings.

FAVORITE SALMON CASSEROLE

1 (1-pound) can salmon
1 onion, sliced
3 tablespoons shortening
3 tablespoons all-purpose flour
1 cup milk
½ teaspoon salt
   Dash pepper
1 cup liquid drained from cooked vegetables and salmon
1 cup cooked carrots
2 cups cooked peas
   Buttered crumbs

Drain salmon, reserving liquid; remove bones and skin. Break salmon in large pieces and place in an oiled 1½-quart baking dish. Sauté onion in melted shortening. Add flour, milk, salt, pepper, and liquid; cook over low heat until slightly thickened. Add carrots and peas; pour over salmon. Top with crumbs and bake at 350° for 30 minutes. Yield: 6 servings.

Hot Coals

Start fire 30 minutes ahead of cooking time so coals will be hot, not blazing. Let frozen fish thaw before cooking on a grill to shorten the cooking time.

SALMON AND POTATO CASSEROLE

2 cups cooked mashed potatoes
1 medium onion, chopped
¾ cup chopped green pepper
2 tablespoons salad oil
1 cup white sauce
1 (17-ounce) can creamed corn
1 (1-pound) can salmon, drained and liquid reserved

Keep cooked mashed potatoes warm. Cook the onion and green pepper in oil for about 10 minutes, or until tender, but not brown. Stir in white sauce, corn, and liquid from the can of salmon. Mix and heat to simmering. Add flaked salmon and heat.
Pour mixture into a 1½-quart casserole dish, and surround with a border of the mashed potatoes. If desired, place under broiler for 2 to 3 minutes. Yield: 4 to 6 servings.

SALMON CHOPS

1 cup flaked salmon
1 cup dry bread crumbs, divided
¼ teaspoon prepared mustard
1 tablespoon freshly squeezed lemon juice
1½ cups thick white sauce
1 egg
   Hot shortening

Mix the salmon, ½ cup bread crumbs, mustard, lemon juice, and white sauce. Place in the refrigerator to cool and set. Shape like chops. Coat with the beaten egg and remaining crumbs and fry in hot shortening until crisp and brown. Yield: 6 servings.

SALMON CHOWDER

1 large onion, diced
2 large potatoes, diced
3 cups water
2 teaspoons salt
1 (17-ounce) can whole kernel corn, drained
1 (1-pound) can red salmon, flaked
4 cups milk
   Salt and pepper to taste

Combine onion, potatoes, water, and salt in saucepan; cook until vegetables are tender. Add corn and salmon and mix well. Slowly stir in milk; add salt and pepper to taste. Heat, but do not let mixture boil. Serve hot.
Yield: 8 to 10 servings.

SALMON CROQUETTES FOR TWO

1 (7¾-ounce) can salmon
¼ teaspoon seasoned salt
¼ teaspoon salt
1 teaspoon freshly squeezed lemon juice
1 egg, beaten
1 tablespoon melted butter or margarine
Few drops Worcestershire sauce
1 cup cornflake crumbs
4 tablespoons melted butter or margarine

The day before serving, drain and remove bones from salmon; break into small pieces with a fork. Add salts, lemon juice, beaten egg, 1 tablespoon melted butter, and the Worcestershire sauce; mix thoroughly. Shape into 4 patties, wrap in plastic wrap or aluminum foil, and place in refrigerator overnight. The next day roll patties in cornflake crumbs and sauté in melted butter until brown on both sides. Yield: 2 servings.

SALMON FLIPS

1 (1-pound) can salmon
4 slices bacon
¾ cup Cheddar cheese soup
1 teaspoon horseradish
1 teaspoon instant minced onion
Dash pepper
1 cup butter or margarine, softened
1 cup shredded cheese
2 cups all-purpose flour
Dash salt
Dash cayenne pepper

Drain and flake salmon. Fry bacon until crisp, drain on absorbent paper, and crumble. Combine salmon, bacon, soup, horseradish, minced onion, and pepper. Prepare pastry by creaming the butter and cheese, adding flour and seasonings, and mixing thoroughly. Shape dough into a ball and chill at least 3 hours.

When the pastry has chilled, roll very thin and cut into 2½-inch squares. Place a heaping teaspoonful of salmon mixture on half of each square. Fold over and press edges together with a fork. Place turnovers on a 15- x 10- x 1-inch baking pan. Prick top to allow steam to escape. Bake at 450° for 10 to 12 minutes or until lightly browned. Yield: about 80 hors d'oeuvres.

Aluminum Foil

Use heavy-duty aluminum foil as a disposable platter for seafood and as bowls for salads, pickles, seasonings, and vegetables.

SALMON LASAGNA

¼ cup chopped onion
⅓ cup chopped green pepper
2 tablespoons butter or margarine
1 (6-ounce) can tomato paste
¾ cup water
½ teaspoon salt
Dash pepper
½ teaspoon basil
2 (7¾-ounce) cans salmon, drained and flaked
¼ pound lasagna noodles, cooked
4 ounces Mozzarella cheese, sliced thin
¼ cup grated Parmesan cheese

Sauté onion and green pepper in butter until tender. Add tomato paste, water, seasonings, and salmon. Layer noodles, salmon mixture, and the cheeses in a 9-inch square pan ending with cheese layer on top. Bake at 375° for 25 to 30 minutes or until browned and bubbly. Yield: 6 servings.

SALMON MILANO

7 slices bread
3 tablespoons butter or margarine
1 (10-ounce) box frozen broccoli spears
1½ tablespoons minced onion
1 cup white sauce
¼ cup milk
½ teaspoon chopped dillweed
1 (1-pound) can salmon, drained and liquid reserved

Toast bread; trim; butter (using 1½ tablespoons of the butter) and cut into triangles. Cook broccoli according to package directions. Drain; add ½ tablespoon butter, and keep warm. Heat remaining butter in a saucepan; add onion and cook for 3 minutes without letting it brown. Add white sauce, milk, dill, and liquid from can of salmon. Add flaked salmon and heat.

Arrange broccoli in an 8½-inch pie plate, reserving one cluster for garnish. Pour salmon mixture over broccoli, arrange toast points around sides of dish, and garnish with the broccoli cluster. Yield: 4 to 6 servings.

Outdoor Fish Fry

Have your fire high with hickory chips. Place lard (not butter) in a heavy iron skillet. Roll fish fillets, steaks, or panfish in cornmeal after sprinkling generously with salt, pepper, and lemon juice. Place fish in hot (not smoking) fat and fry on both sides until golden brown. Remove fish to a hot serving platter, then fry hush puppies (make them small) in the same fat.

SALMON STRIPS

1 (7¾-ounce) can salmon
¼ cup chopped green pepper
¼ cup mayonnaise
3 tablespoons catsup
¼ teaspoon salt
8 thin slices white bread
3 hard-cooked eggs

Drain salmon and remove skin and bones.
Add green pepper, mayonnaise, catsup, and salt,
and blend well. Cut each slice of white bread
into 3 strips and spread with mixture. Press eggs
through ricer or chop very fine. Sprinkle on top of
salmon. Garnish with mayonnaise and set under
broiler for 5 minutes. Serve immediately.
Yield: 24 canapés.

Note: For open-faced luncheon sandwiches,
spread salmon mixture on whole slices of
white bread. Slice hard-cooked eggs onto each
sandwich. Garnish with mayonnaise and broil
as above. Yield: 8 sandwiches.

SALMON CABBAGE VINAIGRETTE

1 (1-pound) can salmon
4 cups shredded cabbage
¼ cup chopped onion
¼ cup chopped parsley
2 hard-cooked eggs, chopped
   Vinaigrette Dressing
18 large cabbage leaves

Drain and flake salmon. Combine cabbage,
onion, parsley, eggs, and salmon. Add Vinaigrette
Dressing and mix thoroughly. Serve in the center
of a cabbage rosette. Yield: 6 servings.

Vinaigrette Dressing

1 teaspoon salt
   Dash cayenne pepper
¼ teaspoon paprika
3 tablespoons vinegar
½ cup olive or salad oil
1 tablespoon chopped pimiento
1 tablespoon chopped sweet pickle
1 tablespoon chopped green pepper

Combine salt, cayenne pepper, and paprika.
Add vinegar and oil slowly, beating thoroughly.
Add pimiento, sweet pickle, and green
pepper. Yield: 6 servings.

CHEESE SALMON LOAF

1 (1-pound) can salmon, drained and flaked
1 egg, beaten
½ cup cream
½ teaspoon salt
⅛ teaspoon pepper
3 tablespoons melted butter or margarine
1 tablespoon freshly squeezed lemon juice
1¼ cups shredded Cheddar cheese
1 cup bread crumbs
   Celery Sauce

Combine all ingredients except bread crumbs
and Celery Sauce and put into a greased loafpan.
Top with buttered bread crumbs and bake at
350° for 30 minutes. Serve hot or cold with
Celery Sauce. Yield: 6 servings.

Celery Sauce

Combine 2 cups well-seasoned white sauce
with 1 cup chopped, cooked celery.

FAVORITE SALMON LOAF AND SAUCE

⅓ cup butter or margarine
½ cup all-purpose flour
2 cups milk
1½ teaspoons salt
¼ teaspoon pepper
1 (1-pound) can salmon, drained
⅓ cup dry bread crumbs
1 tablespoon freshly squeezed lemon juice
2 tablespoons minced onion
½ teaspoon ground nutmeg
2 eggs, well beaten
½ cup milk
1 tablespoon freshly squeezed lemon juice
2 tablespoons chopped parsley
¼ cup mayonnaise

Melt butter in a saucepan over low heat.
Add flour. Add milk gradually and cook over low
heat until thickened. Season with salt and
pepper. Drain salmon, if necessary, and remove
bones. Mix salmon thoroughly with bread crumbs,
lemon juice, onion, nutmeg, eggs, and half the
white sauce. Spoon salmon mixture into a greased
8- x 4- x 3-inch loafpan. Bake at 350° for 30
minutes. To remaining white sauce add ½ cup
milk, lemon juice, and parsley. Heat white
sauce thoroughly and just before serving stir sauce
into mayonnaise; serve hot with Salmon Loaf.
Yield: 6 servings.

SALMON LOAF WITH PIMIENTO MUSHROOM SAUCE

  1 (1-pound) can salmon, drained, boned, and flaked
  1 tablespoon freshly squeezed lemon juice
  3 tablespoons all-purpose flour
  3 tablespoons melted butter or margarine
1½ cups milk
  2 eggs, beaten
  1 cup quick-cooking or regular oats, uncooked
  2 tablespoons minced parsley
 ½ teaspoon salt
    Pimiento Mushroom Sauce

Sprinkle salmon with lemon juice. Stir flour into melted butter; add milk all at once and cook, stirring constantly until thickened. Add salmon, eggs, oats, parsley, and salt; mix carefully. Spoon into a well-greased 9- x 5- x 3-inch loafpan. Bake at 350° until done, about 50 minutes. Serve with Pimiento Mushroom Sauce. Yield: 6 servings.

Pimiento Mushroom Sauce

  1 (10¾-ounce) can cream of mushroom soup, undiluted
 ¼ cup milk
  2 tablespoons chopped pimiento

Combine ingredients; mix. Heat and serve with salmon loaf.

SALMON LOAF WITH SHRIMP SAUCE

  2 (1-pound) cans salmon
 ¼ cup finely minced onion
 ¼ cup chopped parsley
 ¼ cup freshly squeezed lemon juice
 ½ teaspoon salt
 ½ teaspoon pepper
 ½ to 1 teaspoon ground thyme
  2 cups cracker crumbs
 ½ cup milk
  4 eggs, well beaten
 ¼ cup butter or margarine, melted
    Shrimp Sauce

Drain salmon, reserving liquid. Flake salmon into a bowl. Add onion, parsley, lemon juice, seasonings, and cracker crumbs; mix lightly. Add enough milk to salmon liquid to make 1 cup; add liquid, eggs, and melted butter. Mix lightly. Spoon into a greased 9- x 5- x 3-inch loafpan or casserole dish. Bake at 350° for 1 hour or until loaf is set in center. Serve with Shrimp Sauce. Yield: 8 servings.

Shrimp Sauce

Heat 1 (10¾-ounce) can cream of shrimp soup; add ¼ cup milk; stir until smooth. Spoon onto hot loaf.

SALMON RICE SOUFFLE

 ⅓ cup precooked rice
 ⅓ cup water
  2 tablespoons butter or margarine
 ½ teaspoon salt
  1 (7¾-ounce) can salmon, flaked
 ½ cup crushed potato chips
 ⅓ cup milk
1½ cups shredded Cheddar cheese
  7 egg yolks
  7 egg whites

Set a greased 2-quart loafpan in a shallow baking pan; place in oven. Pour boiling water around loafpan to depth of at least 1 inch; let loafpan heat in oven at 350° while preparing soufflé.

Combine rice, water, butter and salt and cook according to package directions. Combine cooked rice, salmon, potato chips, milk, and cheese. Beat egg yolks until thick and lemon-colored; fold into salmon mixture. Beat egg whites until stiff and glossy, but not dry. Fold beaten whites gently into salmon mixture. Pour into hot loafpan. Bake until puffy and delicately browned (a silver knife inserted halfway between center and outside edge should come out clean), about 1 hour. Serve immediately. Yield: 4 to 6 servings.

FAVORITE SALMON MOLD

  1 tablespoon butter or margarine
 ½ tablespoon cornstarch
  1 teaspoon dry mustard
  2 egg yolks
 ¾ cup milk
 ¾ tablespoon unflavored gelatin
  2 tablespoons cold water
 ¼ cup freshly squeezed lemon juice
  1 (1-pound) can salmon, drained
    Salt to taste
 ½ cup whipping cream, whipped
 ½ cup diced cucumber

Cook butter, cornstarch, mustard, egg yolks, and milk in top of double boiler to soft custard consistency. Add gelatin which has been dissolved in cold water. Add lemon juice and salmon. Season to taste. (Rub salmon through coarse sieve if a fine texture is desired.) Cool. Fold in whipped cream and cucumbers. Pour into one large mold or 6 small molds. Yield: 6 servings.

SALMON NUGGETS

1 egg
2 cups seasoned mashed potatoes
2 tablespoons minced parsley
1 (7¾-ounce) can salmon, drained and flaked
  Salt and pepper to taste
½ cup all-purpose flour
2 eggs
2 tablespoons water
2 cups cornflake crumbs
  Parsley sprigs
  Savory Sauce

Beat 1 egg lightly and mix with potatoes, parsley, salmon, salt, and pepper. Form mixture into small balls. Roll balls in flour. Beat 2 eggs lightly with the water. Dip balls into egg mixture, then roll in cornflake crumbs. Fry in deep shortening heated to 365° for about 5 minutes, or until golden brown. Drain well on absorbent paper and keep hot until ready to serve. Or refrigerate or freeze on baking sheets. Reheat at 350° for 15 minutes. When ready to serve, stack the salmon nuggets in a pyramid on the serving plate and garnish with sprigs of parsley. Serve with Savory Sauce. Yield: 4 to 6 servings.

Savory Sauce

1 cup mayonnaise
2 tablespoons chopped parsley
2 tablespoons chopped green onions
2 tablespoons chopped stuffed olives
2 tablespoons chopped dill pickles
½ teaspoon dry mustard
1 teaspoon freshly squeezed lemon juice

Combine all ingredients and serve with the salmon nuggets. Yield: 1½ cups.

SALMON PASTA

1 (1-pound) can salmon
½ pound ricotta cheese
6 lasagna noodles
3 quarts boiling water
1 tablespoon salt
1 (10-ounce) package frozen chopped spinach
¼ cup all-purpose flour
1 teaspoon salt
  Dash pepper
  Dash ground nutmeg
¼ cup melted shortening
1½ cups milk
¼ cup grated Parmesan cheese
  Paprika

Drain and flake salmon. Add ricotta cheese and mix well. Cook noodles in boiling salted water for 30 minutes or until tender; drain. Rinse with hot water. Cook spinach according to package directions; drain. Blend flour and seasonings into shortening. Add milk gradually and cook until thick, stirring constantly. Add spinach and blend thoroughly. Reserve 1 cup of sauce for topping. Pour remaining sauce into a well-greased 8-inch square baking dish. Cut lasagna noodles in half. Place approximately 2 tablespoons salmon mixture in center of each half. Roll each noodle around filling and place, seam side down, in sauce. Pour remaining sauce over top. Sprinkle with Parmesan cheese and paprika. Bake at 350° for 30 minutes. Yield: 6 servings.

SALMON SURPRISE PATTIES

1 (1-pound) can salmon
½ cup mashed potatoes
¼ cup thinly sliced celery
2 tablespoons finely chopped onion
1 egg, beaten
1 teaspoon Worcestershire sauce
¼ teaspoon salt
  Dash pepper
¼ pound sharp process cheese
1 cup crushed cornflakes
  Hot shortening

Drain and flake salmon, removing bones and skin. Combine salmon with next 7 ingredients; mix well. Shape mixture into 8 thin patties. Cut cheese into 4 slices to fit patties; place slice of cheese on each of 4 patties; cover with remaining patties; seal edges. Coat well with cornflake crumbs. Cook in hot shortening over medium heat until golden brown, about 15 minutes, turning once. Yield: 4 servings.

SALMON PIE

2 cups milk
3 eggs
1 envelope cream of leek soup mix
1 (7¾-ounce) can salmon, drained and flaked
1 (9-inch) unbaked pastry shell

Blend milk, eggs, and soup mix with rotary beater. Stir in salmon. Pour into unbaked pastry shell. Bake at 425° for 15 minutes, then set oven temperature control at 350° and continue baking until pastry is golden brown and filling is set, about 30 to 40 minutes longer. Serve warm. Yield: 1 (9-inch) pie.

SALMON-BROCCOLI PIE

- 1 (1-pound) can salmon
- ¼ cup butter or margarine
- ¼ cup all-purpose flour
- ½ teaspoon thyme
- ¼ teaspoon pepper
- 2 cups salmon liquid and milk
- 1 (4-ounce) can chopped mushrooms, drained
- 1 tablespoon chopped parsley
- 1½ cups cooked, drained, chopped broccoli
- 1 cup pastry mix

Drain salmon, reserving liquid. Break salmon into large pieces. Melt butter; blend in flour and seasonings. Add salmon liquid and milk gradually and cook until thick and smooth, stirring constantly. Add mushrooms, parsley, and salmon. Spread broccoli in a 9-inch piepan. Pour salmon mixture over broccoli.

Prepare pastry mix according to package directions. Roll dough to form a 10-inch circle. Place dough over salmon mixture. Double edge of pastry over and pinch with fingers to make an upright rim. Cut top to allow steam to escape. Bake at 425° for 20 to 25 minutes, or until brown. Yield: 6 servings.

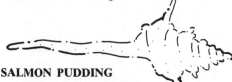

SALMON PUDDING

- 4 medium onions, thinly sliced
- 4 tablespoons butter, margarine, or shortening
- 2 tablespoons all-purpose flour
- 1 (14½-ounce) can evaporated milk
- 1 bay leaf
- 2 teaspoons salt
- ¼ teaspoon pepper
- ½ teaspoon dillseed
- 1 (1-pound) can salmon
- 2 large potatoes, thinly sliced

Cook onions in 2 tablespoons melted butter until limp. Stir occasionally. Heat remaining 2 tablespoons of butter, stir in flour smoothly, and add milk. Cook, stirring constantly, until sauce bubbles. Season with bay leaf, salt, pepper, and dillseed. Drain liquid from salmon and fork into small pieces.

Put a layer of potatoes on the bottom of a greased 1½-quart casserole dish; add a layer of onion, a coating of sauce, and a layer of salmon. Repeat the layers, finishing with onions. Bake at 350° for 1 hour, or until potatoes are tender when tested with a fork. Yield: 6 servings.

SALMON PIQUANT

- 1 clove garlic, minced
- 1 small onion, minced
- 2 tablespoons butter or margarine
- 1 tablespoon all-purpose flour
- 1 (8-ounce) can tomato sauce
- 1 (1-pound) can salmon
- 1 tablespoon freshly squeezed lemon juice
- ½ teaspoon Worcestershire sauce
- 1 dill pickle, finely chopped
  Cooked rice

Sauté garlic and onion in melted butter until limp. Stir in flour as smoothly as possible, then add tomato sauce and cook, stirring constantly, until sauce bubbles. Stir in undrained salmon, lemon juice, Worcestershire sauce, and dill pickle. Stir gently (to keep salmon in sizable pieces) until sauce reaches the boiling point. Serve over rice. Yield: 4 servings.

SALMON NOODLE RING WITH PEAS

- 1 (5-ounce) package wide noodles
- ¼ cup all-purpose flour
- 1 teaspoon salt
- ¼ teaspoon pepper
- ½ teaspoon dry mustard
- ¼ cup melted butter or margarine
- 1 (1-pound) can salmon, drained and liquid reserved
  Light cream or half-and-half
- 1 small onion, grated
- 2 canned pimientos, diced
- 2 tablespoons minced parsley
- 2 eggs, beaten
- 2 (1-pound) cans green peas
- 2 tablespoons butter or margarine

Cook noodles according to package directions; rinse and drain.

Blend flour and seasonings into ¼ cup melted butter. Drain liquid from salmon and add enough light cream to make 2 cups. Add to flour mixture and cook until thickened, stirring constantly. Remove from heat.

Add noodles, onion, pimiento, parsley, and eggs to sauce. Gently stir in salmon, which has been broken into bite-size chunks. Spoon into a buttered ring mold. Bake at 350° for about 45 minutes or until firm. Heat peas and add 2 tablespoons butter. Loosen salmon ring around edges and turn out on a large platter; fill center with peas. Yield: 6 to 8 servings.

SALMON-POTATO SCALLOP

  1 (1-pound) can salmon
 ½ cup chopped onion
 ⅓ cup chopped green pepper
  2 tablespoons butter or margarine
  3 tablespoons all-purpose flour
 ½ teaspoon salt
 ¼ teaspoon basil, crushed
     Dash pepper
1½ cups milk
  3 medium potatoes, cooked and thinly sliced
     Crushed potato chips

Drain and flake salmon. Cook onion and green pepper in butter until tender. Blend in flour, salt, basil, and pepper; add milk and cook, stirring, until mixture boils. Combine sauce and potatoes. Place alternate layers of potatoes and salmon in a 1½-quart casserole dish, beginning and ending with potato chips. Bake at 350° for 30 minutes. Yield: 6 servings.

SALMON SALAD

 ½ cup regular uncooked rice
 ¼ cup French dressing
 ¼ cup mayonnaise
 ½ teaspoon salt
 ¼ teaspoon pepper
  1 tablespoon finely chopped onion
  1 teaspoon horseradish
 ½ teaspoon celery seed
 ½ cup chopped celery
  1 hard-cooked egg, chopped
 ½ cup sliced cucumber
  1 cup flaked cooked salmon

Cook rice according to package directions. Add French dressing to the hot cooked rice (about 1½ cups). Cool to room temperature. Add remaining ingredients; mix lightly. Chill for at least 1 hour before serving. Yield: 6 servings.

BAKED SALMON SALAD

  2 (1-pound) cans salmon
  2 cups thinly sliced celery
  1 cup chopped green pepper
 ½ cup chopped onion
 ½ cup mayonnaise or salad dressing
  1 tablespoon freshly squeezed lemon juice
  2 teaspoons Worcestershire sauce
 ½ teaspoon salt
     Dash pepper
  1 cup coarsely crushed potato chips
     Paprika

Drain salmon; break into large pieces. Combine all ingredients except potato chips and paprika. Place salad in 6 well-greased, individual casserole dishes or 5-ounce custard cups. Top with potato chips. Sprinkle with paprika. Bake at 400° for 15 to 20 minutes, or until lightly browned. Yield: 6 servings.

SALMON CAESAR SALAD

  1 (1-pound) can salmon
  1 clove garlic, peeled and quartered
 ½ cup olive oil or salad oil
1½ cups ½-inch toasted bread cubes
  8 cups mixed salad greens
  1 small onion, thinly sliced
 ½ teaspoon salt
     Dash freshly ground pepper
  1 egg, cooked 1 minute
  2 tablespoons freshly squeezed lemon juice
 ⅓ cup grated Parmesan cheese

Drain salmon; break into large pieces. Add garlic to olive oil and let stand at least 1 hour. Remove garlic from oil. Gradually pour ¼ cup of garlic oil over bread cubes, mixing lightly until all the oil is absorbed. Place salad greens, torn into bite-size pieces, in a large salad bowl. Separate onion slices into rings and add to salad greens. Sprinkle with salt and pepper. Pour remaining garlic oil over greens, tossing lightly. Break egg into salad. Add lemon juice and mix thoroughly. Add cheese, bread cubes, and salmon; toss lightly. Serve immediately. Yield: 6 servings.

MOLDED SALMON SALAD

  1 tablespoon unflavored gelatin
 ¼ cup cold water
1½ cups boiling water
 ¼ cup freshly squeezed lemon juice
  1 teaspoon salt
 ⅓ cup sugar
  1 (1-pound) can salmon, drained and flaked
 ⅓ cup commercial sweet relish
 ⅔ cup diced celery
  2 diced hard-cooked eggs
     Salad greens

Soften gelatin in cold water. Add boiling water and stir until dissolved. Add lemon juice, salt, and sugar. Chill until partially congealed. Add the next 4 ingredients. Turn into a 1-quart mold which has been rinsed in cold water. Chill until firm. Unmold on salad greens. Serve with your favorite dressing. Yield: 8 servings.

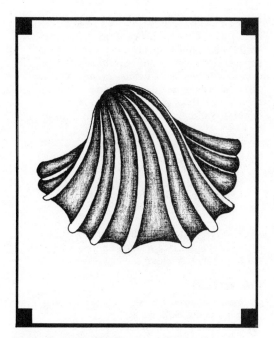

SCALLOPS

It is said that scallops are named for the characteristic scalloped edges of the shells in which they are generally served. These shells are often used for individual baking dishes since they can withstand the heat of the oven.

Bay scallops are small and dainty, have a more delicate flavor than sea scallops, and number about 40 to the pound.

Scallops must be removed from their shells as soon as they are caught. The should then be frozen or iced immediately. Cook scallops quickly, simmering 3 to 5 minutes in liquid (or in less time if they are cooked in hot fat). The part of the scallop which is edible is the adductor muscle, which should have a creamy, mother-of-pearl appearance. Scallops should *never* be boiled.

SCALLOPS AND RICE AU GRATIN

> 1 pound scallops, fresh or frozen
> ¼ cup chopped onion
> ½ cup chopped celery
> ½ cup chopped green pepper
> ¼ cup butter or margarine, melted
> ¼ cup all-purpose flour
> 1 teaspoon salt
>   Dash pepper
> 1 cup milk
> 2 cups cooked rice
> 1 cup shredded cheese

Thaw frozen scallops. Remove any shell particles and coarsely chop. Cook onion, celery, and green pepper in butter until tender. Blend in flour and seasonings. Add milk gradually and cook until thick, stirring constantly. Add scallops. Place one-half the rice in a well-greased 1½-quart casserole dish, cover with one-half the scallop mixture, and one-half the cheese. Repeat. Bake at 350° for 25 to 30 minutes, or until brown. Yield: 6 servings.

SCALLOP BISQUE

> 1 pound scallops, fresh or frozen
> 1 (4-ounce) can mushroom stems and pieces, drained
> ¼ cup butter or margarine, melted
> ½ teaspoon dry mustard
> 1¼ teaspoons salt
>   Dash pepper
> ¼ cup all-purpose flour
> 4 cups milk
>   Paprika

Thaw frozen scallops. Remove any shell particles and wash. Grind scallops and mushrooms. Combine butter, mustard, salt, and pepper. Cook scallop mixture in seasoned butter for 3 to 4 minutes, stirring occasionally. Blend in flour. Add milk gradually and cook until thick, stirring constantly. Serve with paprika sprinkled over the top. Yield: 6 servings.

Skewered Shrimp and Scallops

Shrimp and scallops are tasty when skewered like this: first, mix ⅓ cup prepared mustard, ⅓ cup catsup, ⅓ cup Worcestershire sauce, and dash hot pepper sauce. On long skewers thread in order: mushroom caps, large cooked shrimp, cubes of boiled ham, and tomato quarters. Brush with mustard sauce mixture, roll in cracker crumbs, and brush with melted butter. Grill 12 minutes, turning and basting again.

BOILED SCALLOPS

1 **pound scallops, fresh or frozen**
1 **quart boiling water**
2 **tablespoons salt**

Thaw frozen scallops. Remove any shell particles and wash. Place in boiling salted water. Cover and return to the boiling point. Simmer for 3 to 4 minutes, depending on size. Drain. Yield: 6 servings.

Note: For recipes requiring cooked scallops, 1 pound scallops, fresh or frozen, yields approximately ½ pound cooked scallops.

SCALLOP CANAPES

½ **pound cooked scallops**
2 **cloves garlic, finely chopped**
2 **tablespoons butter or margarine, melted**
½ **cup shredded cheese**
¼ **teaspoon Worcestershire sauce**
Dash salt
Dash pepper
2 **cups commercial pastry mix**

Chop scallops. Cook garlic in butter for 2 to 3 minutes. Add cheese, seasonings, and scallops. Blend well. Prepare pastry mix as directed. Roll very thin and cut into 90 circles, 2 inches in diameter. Place about 1 teaspoon of scallop filling in the center of 45 circles. Cover with remaining 45 circles; press edges together with a fork and vent top. Place on a baking pan and bake at 450° for 10 to 15 minutes, or until brown. Yield: about 45 canapés.

JIFFY SCALLOP CASSEROLE

2 **pounds scallops, fresh or frozen**
1 **quart boiling water**
2 **tablespoons salt**
1 **(1-pound) can cut green beans, drained**
¼ **cup chopped onion**
2 **tablespoons salad oil**
1 **(10¾-ounce) can cream of mushroom soup**
½ **cup milk**
1 **teaspoon curry powder**
Dash pepper
½ **cup cracker crumbs**
¼ **cup shredded cheese**
1 **tablespoon salad oil**

Thaw frozen scallops. Rinse with cold water to remove any shell particles. Place in boiling salted water. Cover and return to the boiling point. Reduce heat and simmer for 3 to 4 minutes, depending on size. Drain. Slice scallops crosswise.

Place beans and scallops in a well-greased baking dish, 8 x 8 x 2 inches. Cook onion in oil until tender. Add soup, milk, curry powder, and pepper. Heat, stirring until well blended. Pour over scallop mixture. Combine crumbs, cheese, and 1 tablespoon salad oil. Sprinkle over top of casserole. Bake at 425° for 15 to 20 minutes. Yield: 6 servings.

SCALLOP COCKTAIL

½ **pound cooked scallops**
Lettuce or salad greens
Cocktail Sauce

Cut large scallops in half. Arrange lettuce in 6 cocktail cups. Place scallops on top; cover with Cocktail Sauce. Yield: 6 servings.

Cocktail Sauce

2 **tablespoons mayonnaise or salad dressing**
2 **tablespoons chili sauce**
2 **tablespoons chopped celery**
1 **tablespoon chopped onion**
¼ **teaspoon salt**
Dash curry powder
Dash pepper

Combine all ingredients and chill. Yield: 6 servings.

Cocktail Sauce

¼ **cup catsup**
2 **tablespoons grated cucumber**
2 **tablespoons grated onion**
¼ **teaspoon salt**
Dash pepper

Combine all ingredients and chill. Yield: 6 servings.

Hickory Smoked Fish

For delicious hickory smoked fish, place a sheet of heavy-duty aluminum foil over outdoor grill and brush with melted fat to prevent fish from sticking. Cook fillets or whole small fish at barbecue adjustment, if using an outdoor stove with hood,* for about 30 minutes. Turn and cook other side. Baste often with melted butter. Serve fish with garlic lemon-butter sauce. Simply melt butter, and add finely minced garlic clove and lemon juice to taste. There will be calls for more.

*If no hood is available, use heavy-duty aluminum foil to improvise a hood.

FRIED SCALLOPS

- 2 pounds scallops, fresh or frozen
- 1 egg, beaten
- 1 tablespoon milk
- 1 teaspoon salt
  Dash pepper
- ½ cup all-purpose flour
- ½ cup dry bread crumbs

Thaw frozen scallops. Remove any shell particles and wash. Cut large scallops in half. Combine egg, milk, and seasonings. Combine flour and crumbs. Dip scallops in egg mixture and roll in flour and crumb mixture.

Panfried

Place scallops in a heavy frying pan which contains about ⅛ inch of salad oil, hot but not smoking. Fry at moderate heat. When scallops are brown on one side, turn carefully and brown the other side. Cooking time is approximately 4 to 6 minutes. Drain on absorbent paper. Yield: 6 servings.

Deep-Fat Fried

Fry scallops in a basket in deep fat at 350° for 2 to 3 minutes or until brown. Drain on absorbent paper. Yield: 6 servings.

PEACHY SCALLOPS

- 1 pound scallops, fresh or frozen
- 2 tablespoons melted butter or margarine
- 2 tablespoons freshly squeezed lemon juice
- ¼ teaspoon salt
  Dash pepper
- 12 canned cling peach halves
- ¼ teaspoon ground cinnamon
- ¼ teaspoon ground cloves
- ¼ teaspoon ground mace
- ¼ teaspoon salt
- 3 slices bacon

Thaw frozen scallops. Rinse with cold water to remove any shell particles. Cut scallops into ½-inch pieces. Combine butter, lemon juce, salt, pepper, and scallops. Place peach halves in a 11- x 7- x 1-inch baking pan. Combine cinnamon, cloves, mace, and salt. Sprinkle over peaches. Place about 2 tablespoons of scallop mixture in center of each peach. Cut bacon into fourths, crosswise. Place a slice on each peach. Broil about 4 inches from source of heat for 8 to 10 minutes or until bacon is crisp. Yield: 6 servings.

SCALLOP-VEGETABLE SALAD

- 1½ pounds scallops, fresh or frozen
- 1 quart boiling water
- 2 tablespoons salt
- 1 (1-pound) can cut green beans, drained
- 1 cup sliced celery
- ¼ cup chopped onion
- ¼ green pepper, chopped
- 1 tablespoon chopped pimiento
  Marinade
- 6 lettuce cups

Thaw frozen scallops. Rinse with cold water to remove any shell particles. Place in boiling salted water. Cover and return to the boiling point. Reduce heat and simmer for 3 to 4 minutes, depending on size. Drain and cool. Slice scallops. Combine all ingredients except lettuce. Cover and chill for at least 1 hour. Drain. Serve in lettuce cups. Yield: 6 servings.

Marinade

- ½ cup cider vinegar
- 1 tablespoon sugar
- ¼ teaspoon salt
  Dash pepper
- ¼ cup salad oil

Combine vinegar, sugar, salt, and pepper. Add oil gradually, blending thoroughly. Yield: about ⅔ cup marinade.

SCALLOP SOUFFLE SNACKS

- ¼ cup mayonnaise or salad dressing
- 2 tablespoons drained sweet pickle relish
- 1 tablespoon chopped parsley
- 1½ teaspoons freshly squeezed lemon juice
- ¼ teaspoon salt
- ¼ teaspoon Worcestershire sauce
  Dash pepper
- 1 pound cooked sea scallops
- 1 egg white, beaten

Combine all ingredients except scallops and egg white. Mix well. Fold into egg white. Place scallops on a well-greased cookie sheet. Top each scallop with mayonnaise mixture. Broil about 3 inches from source of heat for 3 to 4 minutes, or until brown. Yield: about 36 hors d'oeuvres.

Tongs

Use tongs for turning seafood to prevent tearing.

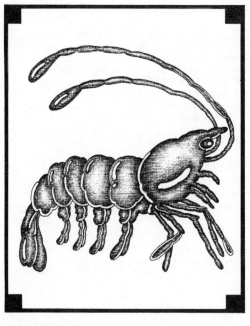

SHRIMP

Shrimp are among the most popular of our shellfish; they are tender and white-meated and have a distinctive flavor. Today they are available fresh, frozen, cooked, canned, and freeze dried.

The various kinds of shrimp marketed include the common shrimp, which varies from a greenish gray to reddish brown, depending upon the location where it was caught. Raw shrimp are often referred to as "green" shrimp.

Shrimp are usually sold according to size or grade, or the number of shrimp per pound. The price varies according to size, which includes the largest or jumbo, 15 to the pound, to the smallest size, which is about 60 to the pound.

Boiling is the basic method of cooking raw shrimp. They may be boiled, then peeled; or they may be peeled, then boiled. More salt is needed if shrimp are boiled before peeling. Bring salted water to a boil, then add shrimp. Bring water again to a boil and simmer for 5 minutes. The time is the same for peeled or unpeeled. After shrimp have cooled, remove shells and sand vein. Wash well and chill immediately.

SHRIMP A LA CREOLE

- 2 tablespoons melted butter or margarine
- 1 tablespoon all-purpose flour
- 2 tablespoons tomato paste
- ½ teaspoon minced onion
- 1 teaspoon salt
- 1 pod hot pepper
- 1½ pints chicken stock
- 2 bay leaves
- ½ teaspoon thyme
- ½ teaspoon minced parsley
- 2 pounds shrimp, deveined
- 3 cups boiled rice

Melt butter; add flour and stir until browned. Add tomato paste, onion, salt, pepper, stock, bay leaves, thyme, and parsley. Cook about 20 minutes; add shrimp and cook 10 minutes longer. Serve with boiled rice or on toast.
Yield: 6 to 8 servings.

SHRIMP IN TOMATO ASPIC

- ¾ pound cooked, peeled, cleaned shrimp
- 2 tablespoons gelatin
- 2 cups tomato juice
- 1 tablespoon freshly squeezed lemon juice
- 1 teaspoon grated onion
- 2 tablespoons chopped pickles
- 2 teaspoons horseradish
- 1 teaspoon salt
  Dash pepper
  Lettuce
  Mayonnaise or salad dressing

Cut large shrimp in half. Soften gelatin in ½ cup cold tomato juice for 5 minutes. Scald remaining tomato juice; add gelatin and stir until dissolved. Add next 6 ingredients and shrimp. Pour in mold. Chill until firm. Unmold on lettuce; garnish with mayonnaise. Yield: 6 servings.

FLORIDA SHRIMP BISQUE

- 2 (10¾-ounce) cans cream of shrimp soup
- 1 (10¾-ounce) can tomato soup
- 3 cups milk
- ⅓ cup sherry (optional)
  Whipped cream
  Onion salt
  Pepper
  Chopped parsley

Combine soups with milk in saucepan. Heat, beating until smooth. Add sherry. Serve topped with whipped cream seasoned with onion salt and pepper. Sprinkle with chopped parsley.
Yield: 6 servings.

SHRIMP BISQUE

¾ pound cooked shrimp
2 tablespoons chopped onion
2 tablespoons chopped celery
¼ cup butter or margarine, melted
2 tablespoons all-purpose flour
1 teaspoon salt
¼ teaspoon paprika
  Dash pepper
4 cups milk
  Chopped parsley

Grind shrimp. Cook onion and celery in butter until tender. Blend in flour and seasonings. Add milk gradually and cook until thick, stirring constantly. Add shrimp; heat. Garnish with chopped parsley. Yield: 6 servings.

EASY SHRIMP ASPIC

½ pound cooked, peeled, cleaned shrimp,
    fresh or frozen
        or
2 (4½- or 5-ounce) cans shrimp
1 (3-ounce) package lemon-flavored gelatin
½ teaspoon salt*
1 cup boiling water
1 (8-ounce) can tomato sauce
1½ tablespoons vinegar
1 teaspoon horseradish
1 teaspoon grated onion
  Dash celery salt
  Salad greens
1 avocado, peeled and sliced
  Sour Cream Dressing

Thaw frozen shrimp or drain canned shrimp. Cover canned shrimp with ice water and let stand for 5 minutes; drain. Cut shrimp into ½-inch pieces. Dissolve gelatin and salt in boiling water. Add tomato sauce, vinegar, horseradish, onion, celery salt, and shrimp; mix thoroughly. Pour into 6 individual ½-cup molds or custard cups; chill until firm. Unmold on salad greens. Garnish with avocado slices and top each serving with approximately 1 tablespoon Sour Cream Dressing. Yield: 6 servings.
* Omit salt if using canned shrimp.

Sour Cream Dressing

⅓ cup commercial sour cream
1 tablespoon freshly squeezed lemon juice
½ teaspoon horseradish
¼ teaspoon salt

Combine all ingredients and mix thoroughly. Chill. Yield: ⅓ cup dressing.

SOY-BARBECUED SHRIMP

2 pounds fresh shrimp
2 cloves garlic
½ teaspoon salt
½ cup soy sauce
½ cup freshly squeezed lemon juice
3 tablespoons finely chopped parsley
2 teaspoons dehydrated onion flakes
½ teaspoon pepper

Shell and devein shrimp, leaving tails on. Arrange shrimp in shallow dish. Mash garlic in small bowl with salt. Make marinade by stirring in remaining ingredients. Pour marinade over shrimp and thread shrimp on skewers. Grill 3 minutes, basting with marinade. Turn. Grill 5 minutes more, basting several times. Use any remaining marinade as dip. Yield: 4 servings.

CHARCOAL BROILED SHRIMP

1 cup olive oil
½ cup minced onion
2 cloves garlic, minced
¼ cup freshly squeezed lemon juice
3 shallots, finely chopped
¼ cup finely chopped parsley
1½ pounds large raw shrimp, peeled and
    deveined (about 2 pounds in shell)

Combine olive oil, onion, garlic, lemon juice, shallots, and parsley for a marinade. Put in a large flat dish; add shrimp. Marinade in refrigerator for several hours, turning shrimp often. Remove shrimp from marinade and drain. Divide shrimp evenly on 8 to 10 squares of heavy-duty aluminum foil. Seal foil and cook over medium hot coals for about 6 to 8 minutes; turn foil packets and cook 6 to 8 minutes on other side. Serve at once. Yield: 8 to 10 servings.

QUICK BROILED SHRIMP

1½ pounds shrimp (large)
¼ cup butter or margarine
1 clove garlic, crushed

Shell shrimp and devein. Heat butter with garlic. Dip shrimp in butter mixture. Broil 3 minutes on each side. Yield: 30 appetizers.
Variation: Dip shrimp into 2 tablespoons lemon juice mixed with ½ teaspoon seasoned salt and ⅛ teaspoon pepper. Fold a half slice of bacon around each shrimp; fasten with short toothpick. Broil for 5 minutes on each side or until bacon is crisp and shrimp is tender. Yield: 30 appetizers.

CAROLINA SHRIMP CASSEROLE

⅓ cup salad oil
½ cup chopped onion
2 pounds fresh shrimp shelled and deveined;
   or 2 pounds thawed frozen shrimp
1 teaspoon Worcestershire sauce
½ teaspoon paprika
   Dash cayenne pepper
   Salt to taste
4 cups cooked rice
3 slices bacon

Heat oil in a skillet; add onions and cook for 5 minutes. Stir in shrimp and seasonings and cook for 5 minutes. Add rice; mix well and turn into an ungreased 1½-quart casserole dish. Top with bacon. Bake at 375° for 25 minutes, or until bacon is crisp. Yield: 6 to 8 servings.

SHRIMP-CORN CASSEROLE

3 tablespoons butter or margarine
3 tablespoons all-purpose flour
1½ cups milk
¾ cup crumbled blue cheese (about 4 ounces)
2 (12-ounce) cans whole kernel corn, drained
1 tablespoon grated onion
½ teaspoon celery seed
¼ teaspoon onion salt
1 pound shrimp, cooked, shelled, and deveined
   Parsley

Melt butter. Add flour and blend. Gradually add milk and cook over low heat, stirring constantly, until thickened. Add cheese and cook, stirring constantly, until cheese is melted. Add corn, onion, seasonings, and half of shrimp. Mix well. Turn into a greased 1½-quart baking dish. Top with remaining shrimp, and bake at 350° for 30 minutes. Garnish with parsley. Yield: 4 to 6 servings.

SHRIMP DINNER CASSEROLE

1 cup diced celery
1½ cups chopped green onions with tops
3 cloves garlic, minced
⅓ cup butter or margarine
1 (10¾-ounce) can cream of mushroom soup
½ cup water
3 tablespoons minced parsley
3 cups cooked rice
2 slices bread, moistened
1 teaspoon salt
¼ teaspoon pepper
1 pound peeled and deveined shrimp, halved
¾ cup buttered bread crumbs

Cook celery, onion and garlic in butter until tender. Add soup, water, parsley, rice, and bread. Cook about 10 minutes. Add seasonings and shrimp. Pour into a greased 2½-quart casserole dish. Top with buttered crumbs. Bake at 375° for 30 minutes. Yield: 6 servings.

SHRIMP AND GREEN BEAN CASSEROLE

3 (4½- or 5-ounce) cans shrimp
1 (10-ounce) package frozen French-style green beans
1 (10¾-ounce) can cream of celery soup
2 tablespoons chopped parsley
1 teaspoon freshly squeezed lemon juice
1 teaspoon grated onion
½ teaspoon grated lemon rind
½ cup shredded Cheddar cheese
   Paprika

Drain shrimp and rinse with cold water. Cook green beans according to directions on package, omitting salt. Drain thoroughly. Place beans in a well-greased, shallow 1½-quart casserole dish. Cover with shrimp. Combine soup, parsley, lemon juice, onion, and lemon rind. Pour over shrimp. Top with cheese. Sprinkle with paprika. Bake at 350° for 20 to 25 minutes or until cheese melts and is lightly browned. Yield: 6 servings.

SHRIMP AND OYSTER CASSEROLE

3 pounds shrimp
36 shell oysters
½ cup oyster liquor
¼ cup butter or margarine
⅓ cup all-purpose flour
1 cup light cream
½ cup white wine
2 cups grated Swiss or Gruyère cheese
2 (6-ounce) cans sliced mushrooms, drained
1 teaspoon crumbled dillweed
   Salt and pepper
½ cup cornflake crumbs

Cook shrimp; shell, and devein. Shuck oysters, reserving ½ cup of the liquor. Melt butter in skillet; stir in flour. Gradually stir in oyster liquor, cream, and wine. Cook, stirring until sauce becomes smooth and thickens. Stir in 1 cup of the cheese. Add shrimp, oysters, mushrooms, and dill. Simmer for 5 minutes, stirring constantly. Season to taste with salt and pepper. Pour mixture into a shallow, greased casserole dish; top with cornflake crumbs mixed with remaining cheese. Broil until golden and bubbly. Yield: 8 to 10 servings.

SAUCY SHRIMP CASSEROLE

¼ cup butter or margarine
¼ cup all-purpose flour
2 cups milk
1 teaspoon salt
½ teaspoon Worcestershire sauce
1 (8-ounce) wedge Cheddar cheese, shredded
6 hard-cooked eggs, sliced
2½ cups (1 pound) cooked shrimp
Paprika (optional)
Parsley (optional)

Make cream sauce with butter, flour, milk, and seasonings. Add cheese, stirring until melted. Alternate layers of egg slices, shrimp, and sauce in 1½-quart casserole dish. Bake at 350° for 20 to 25 minutes. Garnish with paprika and parsley, if desired. Yield: 6 servings.

CANTONESE SHRIMP AND BEANS

1½ pounds frozen raw, peeled, deveined shrimp
1½ teaspoons chicken stock base
1 cup boiling water
¼ cup thinly sliced green onion
1 clove garlic, crushed
1 tablespoon salad oil
1 teaspoon salt
½ teaspoon ground ginger
Dash pepper
1 (10-ounce) package frozen cut green beans
1 tablespoon cornstarch
1 tablespoon cold water

Thaw frozen shrimp. Dissolve chicken stock base in boiling water. Sauté onion, garlic, and shrimp in oil for 3 minutes, stirring frequently. If necessary, add a little of the chicken broth to prevent sticking. Stir in salt, ginger, pepper, green beans, and chicken broth. Cover and simmer 5 to 7 minutes longer or until beans are cooked but still slightly crisp. Combine cornstarch and water. Add cornstarch mixture to shrimp and cook until thick and clear, stirring constantly. Yield: 6 servings.

SHRIMP SEVICHE

1 pound shrimp, cooked and deveined
Juice of 4 limes or enough to cover shrimp
2 tablespoons grated onion
2 tablespoons minced green pepper
1 fresh tomato, finely chopped
½ cup tomato juice
Salt, pepper, and hot pepper sauce to taste

Soak shrimp in lime juice 1 hour or more in refrigerator. Stir and drain. Combine lime juice with other ingredients. Serve in small bowls as a sauce for shrimp used as appetizers. Yield: 4 to 6 servings.

SHRIMP COCKTAIL

2 pounds boiled shrimp
½ cup olive oil
¼ cup paprika
1 tablespoon horseradish
1 tablespoon prepared mustard
¼ cup tarragon vinegar
1 teaspoon celery seed
½ teaspoon salt
⅛ teaspoon pepper
½ teaspoon onion salt
Dash hot pepper sauce

Chill shrimp and place in cocktail cups on cracked ice. Combine other ingredients and serve in small container centered on ice. Yield: 6 servings.

SHRIMP AND PEPPER COMBO

1 pound fresh medium shrimp, cleaned
1 (6-ounce) jar red peppers
1 medium or large green pepper, cut into 1-inch squares
Barbecue Sauce

Pierce shrimp through rounded side with skewer, alternating shrimp on skewer with pieces of red and green pepper. Brush with Barbecue Sauce. Place on lower rack of grill and cook at medium heat until shrimp turn golden brown (about 8 to 10 minutes). Turn skewers at least once and baste frequently while cooking. Yield: 4 to 6 servings.

Barbecue Sauce

½ cup pineapple juice
2 teaspoons brown sugar
2 teaspoons freshly squeezed lemon juice
1 teaspoon soy sauce

Combine ingredients and use as basting sauce for Shrimp and Pepper Combo. Yield: ½ cup sauce.

SHRIMP CREOLE

- 2 medium onions, sliced
- 1 cup chopped celery (about 4 stalks)
- ¼ cup chopped green pepper
- 4 tablespoons shortening
- 2 tablespoons all-purpose flour
- 1 teaspoon salt
- 2 tablespoons chili powder
- 2 cups canned tomatoes
- 1 tablespoon vinegar
- 1 pound cooked shrimp
- 1 cup cooked peas
  Hot cooked rice

Brown onion, celery, and green pepper in shortening. Blend in flour, salt, and chili powder. Add tomatoes and vinegar; simmer for 15 minutes. Add shrimp and peas and cook for 1 minute. Serve over rice. Yield: 6 to 8 servings.

GULF SHRIMP CREOLE

- 1½ pounds shrimp, fresh or frozen
- ¼ cup chopped onion
- ¼ cup chopped green pepper
- 1 clove garlic, finely chopped
- ¼ cup butter or margarine, melted
- 3 tablespoons all-purpose flour
- 1 teaspoon chili powder
  Dash pepper
- 1 teaspoon salt
- 2 cups canned tomatoes
  Ring of cooked rice

Peel shrimp, devein, and wash. Cut large shrimp in half. Cook onion, green pepper, and garlic in butter until tender. Blend in flour and seasonings. Add tomatoes and cook until thick, stirring constantly. Add shrimp and simmer uncovered for about 20 minutes. Serve in a ring of cooked rice. Yield: 6 servings.

SOUTHERN SHRIMP CREOLE

- 1 pound shrimp, boiled, shelled, and deveined
- 1 cup chopped onion
- 1 cup chopped green peper
- 1 cup chopped celery
- 2 tablespoons bacon drippings
- 1 tablespoon Worcestershire sauce
  Few dashes hot pepper sauce
- 1 teaspoon salt
- ½ teaspoon pepper
- 1 quart fresh, chopped tomatoes

Prepare shrimp; if large shrimp are used, cut in half. Sauté shrimp, onion, pepper, and celery in bacon drippings. Add other ingredients and put in a 2½-quart baking dish and bake at 450° for about 15 minutes. Yield: 6 servings.

CRUSTY SHRIMP

- ½ pound cooked, peeled, cleaned shrimp, fresh or frozen
  or
- 2 (4½-ounce) cans shrimp
- 3 tablespoons mayonnaise or salad dressing
- 2 tablespoons freshly squeezed lemon juice
- 1 tablespoon chopped sweet pickle
- 1 teaspoon horseradish
- 1 teaspoon prepared mustard
- 1 teaspoon salt
  Pastry for 1 (9-inch) piecrust
  Paprika

Thaw and drain frozen shrimp; rinse with cold water. Grind. Combine all ingredients except pastry and paprika. Mix thoroughly. Roll pastry very thin and cut in 2½-inch circles. Place a teaspoonful of shrimp mixture in the center of each circle. Moisten edges with cold water. Fold over and press edges together with a fork. Place turnovers on a 15- x 10- x 1-inch baking pan. Prick top to allow steam to escape. Sprinkle with paprika. Bake at 450° for 12 to 15 minutes, or until lightly browned. Yield: about 40 hors d'oeuvres.

SHRIMP DE JONGHE

- 4 (4½- or 5-ounce) cans shrimp
- ¾ cup toasted dry bread crumbs
- ¼ cup chopped green onions and tops
- ¼ cup chopped parsley
- ¾ teaspoon crushed tarragon
- ¼ teaspoon crushed garlic
- ¼ teaspoon ground nutmeg
- ¼ teaspoon salt
  Dash pepper
- ½ cup butter or margarine, melted
- ¼ cup sherry

Drain shrimp. Cover shrimp with ice water and let stand for 5 minutes; drain. Combine crumbs, onion, parsley, and seasonings. Add butter and sherry; mix thoroughly. Combine crumb mixture and shrimp; toss lightly. Place in a well-greased, shallow 1-quart casserole dish. Bake at 400° for 15 to 20 minutes, or until lightly browned. Yield: 6 servings.

CURRIED SHRIMP

¾ pound cooked shrimp
¼ cup chopped onion
 3 tablespoons butter or margarine
 3 tablespoons all-purpose flour
 1 teaspoon salt
    Dash pepper
 1 teaspoon curry powder
¼ teaspoon ground ginger
 2 cups milk
    Ring of cooked rice

Cut large shrimp in half. Cook onion in butter until tender. Blend in flour and seasonings. Add milk gradually and cook until thick, stirring constantly. Add shrimp; heat. Serve in ring of cooked rice. Yield: 6 servings.

SHRIMP CURRY

 2 pounds shrimp
½ cup butter or margarine
 1 large onion, sliced
 1 clove garlic, minced
 3 stalks celery, sliced diagonally
½ cup all-purpose flour
 3 cups milk
 1 small green pepper, cut into thin strips
 1 teaspoon salt
¼ teaspoon white pepper
¼ teaspoon cayenne pepper
¼ teaspoon turmeric
 2 tablespoons curry powder
 2 tablespoons freshly squeezed lemon juice
    Rice and condiments

Remove shells and veins from shrimp; split lengthwise. Melt butter in large skillet and sauté shrimp until light pink; add onion, garlic, and celery; cook until limp. Lower heat and stir in flour to coat ingredients. Add milk, stirring until smooth. Add green pepper and seasonings; cook until thickened, stirring occasionally. Stir in lemon juice. Serve with rice and condiments such as chopped peanuts, green onions, hard-cooked eggs, coconut, and chutney. Yield: 6 servings.

Weight Tablecloth

Weight your picnic tablecloth by sewing small metal washers or fishing sinkers in the hem of each corner.

Apron

Another handy item is an apron with a wide pocket across the top. Attach to tablecloth to hold small items.

TALLAHASSEE SHRIMP DIP

½ pound cooked, peeled, and cleaned shrimp, fresh or frozen
 1 (1⅜- or 1¾-ounce) package onion soup mix
 2 cups commercial sour cream
¼ cup catsup
 1 tablespoon chopped parsley
    Chopped parsley for garnish
    Assorted crackers

Thaw shrimp if frozen and chop. Combine all ingredients except parsley for garnish and crackers. Mix thoroughly. Chill. Garnish with chopped parsley and serve with crackers. Yield: approximately 3¼ cups dip.

DEVILED SHRIMP

 3 tablespoons butter or margarine, melted
 4 tablespoons all-purpose flour
1½ cups milk
 3 hard-cooked eggs, chopped
1½ cups cooked shrimp
 1 tablespoon chopped parsley
 1 tablespoon minced celery
    Few drops onion juice
    Buttered bread crumbs
    Paprika

Combine butter and flour; stir until smooth. Add milk and cook over low heat; continue to stir until thickened. Add eggs and shrimp; stir well. Add parsley, celery, and onion juice. Put mixture into buttered ramekins and top with bread crumbs. Bake at 375° for 10 minutes, or until crumbs are lightly browned. Sprinkle with paprika. Yield: 4 to 6 servings.

SHRIMP FLORENTINE

 1 small onion, chopped
 1 tablespoon butter or margarine
 1 (27-ounce) can spinach, drained
 2 (4½- to 5-ounce) cans small shrimp
 1 (10¾-ounce) can cream of mushroom soup
 3 tablespoons light cream or half-and-half
⅛ teaspoon ground nutmeg
    Grated Parmesan cheese

Cook onion in butter until just tender. Mix in spinach and spoon into greased individual shallow baking dishes. Drain shrimp and rinse in cold water. Arrange on top of spinach mixture. Blend soup, cream, and nutmeg; pour over shrimp and sprinkle with Parmesan cheese. Bake at 425° for 20 minutes. Yield: 4 servings.

FRENCH FRIED SHRIMP

1½ pounds shrimp, fresh or frozen
 2 eggs, beaten
 1 teaspoon salt
 ½ cup all-purpose flour
 ½ cup dry bread crumbs
    Hot shortening

Peel shrimp, leaving last section of shell on if desired. Cut almost through lengthwise and devein. Wash. Combine egg and salt. Dip each shrimp in egg, then roll in flour-and-crumb mixture. Fry in a basket in hot shortening, 350°, for 2 to 3 minutes, or until golden brown. Yield: 6 servings.

HERBED SHRIMP

 2 pounds uncooked shrimp in shells
    or
 1 pound cooked, shelled shrimp
    or
 1 pound canned deveined shrimp
 1 cup butter or margarine
 ½ teaspoon salt
 ¼ teaspoon pepper
 1 teaspoon basil, crushed
 1 teaspoon tarragon, crushed
 1 clove garlic, minced
 1 cup fine dry bread crumbs

Cook shrimp; remove shells and devein. Divide shrimp between 4 to 6 individual shells or casseroles. Cream butter and stir in remaining ingredients. Mix well. Spread crumb mixture over shrimp. Bake at 350° until thoroughly heated, about 20 minutes. Yield: 4 to 6 servings.

SHRIMP AND CORN IN FOIL

 4 cups fresh sweet corn cut from cob
    (about 8 ears)
 ½ teaspoon sugar
1½ teaspoons salt
 ¼ teaspoon onion salt
    Pinch pepper
 1 pound fresh shrimp, peeled
 4 teaspoons freshly squeezed lemon juice
 ¼ cup butter or margarine

Mix cut corn with sugar, salt, onion salt, and pepper. Mix shrimp with lemon juice and add to corn. Place mixture on 4 to 5 squares of heavy-duty aluminum foil and dot liberally with butter. Close foil packages carefully. Place on grill and cook from 10 to 20 minutes. Yield: 4 to 5 servings.

GOLDEN SHRIMP

1½ cups all-purpose flour
 1 teaspoon baking powder
 ¼ teaspoon salt
 2 eggs, well beaten
1⅔ cups undiluted evaporated milk
1½ pounds shrimp, shelled and deveined
2½ cups 3-Minute Cheese Sauce

Sift together flour, baking powder, and salt. Add eggs and evaporated milk. Blend. Dip shrimp in batter and cook in hot shortening (375°) for 8 to 10 minutes, or until lightly browned. Drain on absorbent paper. Serve with 3-Minute Cheese Sauce. Yield: 6 servings.

3-Minute Cheese Sauce

1⅔ cups undiluted evaporated milk
 ½ teaspoon salt
 2 teaspoons dry mustard
 2 cups (about 8 ounces) shredded pasteurized
    process American cheese

Simmer evaporated milk, salt, and mustard in saucepan over medium heat to just below boiling, about 2 minutes. Add cheese; stir over medium heat until cheese melts, about 1 minute longer. Yield: 2½ cups.

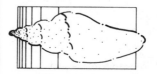

SHRIMP IN SOUR CREAM

 1 pound cooked, peeled, and cleaned shrimp,
    fresh or frozen
    or
 4 (4½- or 5-ounce) cans shrimp
 1 (4-ounce) can sliced mushrooms, drained
 2 tablespoons chopped green onion
 2 tablespoons butter or margarine, melted
 1 tablespoon all-purpose flour
 1 (10¾-ounce) can cream of shrimp soup
 1 cup commerical sour cream
    Dash pepper
    Toast points

Thaw frozen shrimp or drain canned shrimp. Rinse canned shrimp with cold water. Cut large shrimp in half. Cook mushrooms and onion in butter until tender. Blend in flour. Add soup and cook until thickened, stirring constantly. Add sour cream, pepper, and shrimp. Heat, stirring occasionally. Serve on toast points. Yield: 6 servings.

SHRIMP GUMBO

 2 cups sliced fresh okra or 1 (10-ounce)
    package frozen okra, sliced
⅓ cup shortening, melted
⅔ cup chopped green onions and tops
 3 cloves garlic, finely chopped
1½ teaspoons salt
½ teaspoon pepper
 1 (1-pound) package (raw or frozen),
    fully peeled, deveined shrimp
 2 cups hot water
 1 cup canned tomatoes
 2 whole bay leaves
 6 drops hot pepper sauce
1½ cups cooked rice

Sauté okra in shortening about 10 minutes, or until okra appears dry, stirring constantly. Add onion, garlic, salt, pepper, and shrimp. Cook about 5 minutes. Add water, tomatoes, and bay leaves. Cover and simmer for 20 minutes. Remove bay leaves. Add hot pepper sauce. Place ¼ cup rice in the bottom of each of 6 soup bowls; fill with gumbo. Yield: 6 servings.

SOUTHERN SHRIMP JAMBALAYA

¾ pound cooked, peeled, cleaned shrimp,
    fresh or frozen
¼ cup chopped bacon
 3 tablespoons chopped onion
 3 tablespoons chopped green pepper
 1 clove garlic, finely chopped
 1 tablespoon all-purpose flour
½ teaspoon salt
½ teaspoon Worcestershire sauce
    Dash cayenne pepper
    Dash paprika
½ cup pitted ripe olives, sliced crosswise
 1 (16-ounce) can tomatoes
 2 cups cooked rice

Thaw shrimp if frozen; cut large shrimp in half. Fry bacon until crisp. Add onion, green pepper, and garlic; cook until tender. Blend in flour and seasonings; add olives and tomatoes and cook until thick, stirring constantly. Stir in rice and shrimp; heat. Yield: 6 servings.

SHRIMP MIAMI

 2 pounds shrimp, fresh or frozen
¼ cup olive or salad oil
 2 teaspoons salt
½ teaspoon white pepper
¼ cup extra dry vermouth
 2 tablespoons freshly squeezed lemon juice

Thaw shrimp if frozen. Peel shrimp, leaving the last section of the shell on. Devein and wash. Cook shrimp with oil, salt, and pepper in an electric frying pan at 325° for 8 to 10 minutes or until shrimp are pink and tender, stirring frequently. Increase temperature to 425°. Add vermouth and lemon juice. Cook 1 minute longer, stirring constantly. Drain. Serve hot or cold as an appetizer or as an entrée. Yield: 6 servings.

SHRIMP MARENGO

3½ pounds shrimp
 7 slices bacon
 1 clove garlic, crushed
 1 pound mushrooms, wiped and sliced, or
 2 (8-ounce) cans mushroom pieces
 1 medium onion, chopped
 2 (1-pound) cans Italian tomatoes
 1 (6-ounce) can tomato paste
 1 (10½-ounce) can consommé
1½ teaspoons oregano
1½ teaspoons basil
 1 tablespoon sugar
 1 tablespoon salt
⅛ teaspoon pepper
 3 drops hot pepper sauce
6-7 teaspoons prepared mustard
¼ cup all-purpose flour
½ cup water

Cook shrimp 7 minutes in a large amount of boiling water. Shell and devein shrimp. Cut bacon into small pieces and cook until crisp; remove bacon. Sauté shrimp in bacon drippings to which crushed garlic has been added. Add mushrooms and onion and continue to sauté for a few minutes longer. Add tomatoes, tomato paste, bacon, and consommé.

Season with oregano, basil, sugar, salt, pepper, hot pepper sauce, and mustard. Cook 10 minutes, stirring often; taste for seasoning and correct if needed. Mix flour with water until smooth. Add to shrimp mixture, stirring briskly, and let cook about 1 minute.
Yield: 2½ quarts or 10 servings.

NEPTUNE INTERNATIONALE

    1 (8-ounce) package egg noodles
    1 (10¾-ounce) can cream of shrimp soup
 1½ cups milk
    ½ pound shrimp, cooked
    1 (7¾-ounce) can crabmeat, flaked
    1 (4-ounce) can water chestnuts
    1 (8-ounce) can button mushrooms
    1 teaspoon salt
    ½ teaspoon pepper
    3 green onions, chopped
    ½ cup Chablis
    ¼ cup slivered almonds
    ½ cup shredded Cheddar cheese

Cook noodles according to package directions; drain and rinse. Combine soup with milk and heat over medium heat, stirring constantly, until smooth. Remove from heat; add shrimp, crab, sliced water chestnuts, mushrooms, salt, pepper, and green onions. Alternate noodles and creamed mixture in layers in an greased 2½-quart casserole dish. Pour Chablis over all and top with almonds and cheese. Bake at 350° for 35 minutes. Yield: 6 servings.

SHRIMP PIE

 ¾ pound cooked shrimp
    1 chicken bouillon cube
    1 cup boiling water
    1 (10¾-ounce) can cream of mushroom soup
    3 tablespoons chopped onion
    ¼ cup chopped green pepper
    ½ cup chopped celery
    ¼ cup butter or margarine, melted
    ⅓ cup all-purpose flour
    ¾ teaspoon salt
    2 cups pastry mix
    1 tablespoon milk

Cut shrimp in half. Dissolve bouillon cube in boiling water. Add soup, stirring until smooth. Cook onion, green pepper, and celery in butter until tender. Blend in flour and salt. Add bouillon-soup mixture gradually and cook until thick, stirring constantly. Add shrimp; heat. Prepare pastry mix as directed on package. Roll a little more than half of dough very thin and cut into six circles, each 5 inches in diameter. Line six individual 4-inch piepans with pastry. Fill with shrimp mixture. Roll remaining dough. Cut into six circles each 4 inches in diameter. Moisten edges of lower crusts. Place top crusts over shrimp mixture. Seal edges and prick tops. Brush with milk. Bake at 450° for 20 minutes or until brown. Yield: 6 servings.

SHRIMP-ON-A-SKEWER

 ⅓ cup salad oil
    ⅓ cup freshly squeezed lemon juice
    3 or 4 cloves garlic, minced
 1½ teaspoons salt
    ½ teaspoon paprika
    ¼ teaspoon pepper
    2 pounds (about 30 large) fresh or frozen
       shrimp, cleaned
    2 medium green peppers, cut into wedges
    2 medium onions, cut into wedges
 12 red cherry tomatoes or 3 medium tomatoes,
       quartered
       Lemon wedges

Combine salad oil, lemon juice, garlic, and seasonings; pour over shrimp and refrigerate at least 2 hours. Drain, reserving marinade. On 6 greased, 12-inch skewers, alternate shrimp, green pepper, and onion; brush with marinade. Broil 3 inches from heat about 13 minutes, or until shrimp are tender, turning once and brushing frequently with marinade. During last 2 or 3 minutes, place tomatoes on skewers. Serve with lemon wedges. Yield: 6 servings.

SHRIMP PARMESAN

 1½ pounds raw shrimp, shelled and deveined
    ¼ cup all-purpose flour
    1 teaspoon salt
    ⅛ teaspoon pepper
    1 egg
    2 tablespoons freshly squeezed lemon juice
    ½ cup cracker crumbs or bread crumbs
    ½ cup grated Parmesan cheese
       Hot salad oil

Lightly coat shrimp with flour, salt, and pepper. Dip into egg, beaten with lemon juice, then in mixture of cracker crumbs and grated Parmesan cheese. Fry in 1-inch-deep salad oil in skillet for 3 to 5 minutes. Drain and serve on platter garnished with mixed salad greens. Yield: 4 servings.

Butterfly Style: For a butterfly style or fantail shrimp, shell, leaving on last section and tail. Cut down back of shrimp, almost but not completely through. Remove sand vein. Spread shrimp open to lie flat. Fry as above.

Marinated Shrimp: Crush 2 cloves garlic; blend with ½ cup lime or lemon juice. Pour over shrimp. Marinate overnight or several hours. Remove from marinade and fry as above.

SHRIMP MEAL-IN-A-DISH

- 1 **pound shrimp, fresh or frozen**
- ½ **cup butter or margarine**
- ½ **cup thinly sliced onions**
- ⅓ **cup all-purpose flour**
- ½ **teaspoon salt**
  - **Dash pepper**
- 3 **cups milk**
- 1 **cup cooked carrots**
- 1 **cup cooked peas**
- 1 **(8-ounce) package refrigerated biscuits**

Shell and devein shrimp and cut in chunks, reserving 3 whole shrimp for garnish. Melt butter in large skillet or saucepan. Add onion and cook slowly until tender. Sprinkle with flour, salt, and pepper, then gradually stir in milk over low heat. Cook, stirring constantly, until sauce thickens. Fold in carrots, peas, and shrimp. Pour into a greased 1½-quart casserole dish. Arrange biscuits on top in circle. Place 3 shrimp in center of circle. Bake at 450° for 12 to 15 minutes or until biscuits are well browned and shrimp are pink. Yield: 6 servings.

SHRIMP PIZZA

- 3 **(4½- or 5-ounce) cans shrimp**
- ⅓ **cup chopped onion**
- 3 **cloves garlic, finely chopped**
- ½ **cup melted shortening or salad oil**
- 3 **(6-ounce) cans Italian-style tomato paste**
- ⅓ **cup chopped parsley**
- 1½ **teaspoons oregano**
- 3 **(9-inch) unbaked pizza crusts**
- ¾ **pound Mozzarella cheese, thinly sliced**

Drain shrimp and rinse with cold water. Cook onion and garlic in shortening until tender. Add tomato paste and simmer for 5 minutes. Remove from heat; add parsley and oregano. Place pizza crusts on well-greased baking pans. Cover each crust with ⅓ of the sauce, ⅓ of the shrimp, and ⅓ of the cheese. Bake at 425° for 20 minutes, or until crust is brown and cheese melts. Yield: 6 servings.

SHRIMP ORIENTAL

- 1 **pound raw, peeled, deveined shrimp, fresh or frozen**
- ¼ **cup freshly squeezed lemon juice**
- 1 **cup all-purpose flour**
- 3 **eggs, beaten**
- 1½ **teaspoons salt**
  - **Shortening**

Thaw shrimp if frozen. Pour lemon juice over shrimp and let stand 10 minutes. Cut shrimp almost through lengthwise and spread open. Place flour in paper bag; add shrimp and shake well. Combine egg and salt. Dip each shrimp in egg. Place shrimp in a heavy frying pan which contains about ⅛ inch of shortening, hot but not smoking. Fry at moderate heat. When shrimp are brown on one side, turn carefully and brown on other side. Cooking time is approximately 4 minutes. Drain on absorbent paper. Yield: 6 servings.

PEPPERED SHRIMP AND EGGS

- ½ **pound cooked, peeled, and cleaned shrimp, fresh or frozen**
  - **or**
- 2 **(4½-ounce) cans shrimp**
- 3 **slices bacon**
- ¾ **cup chopped green pepper**
- ½ **cup chopped onion**
- ½ **teaspoon salt**
- ¼ **teaspoon cayenne pepper**
- 6 **eggs, beaten**
- ¼ **cup coffee cream**
- ½ **teaspoon Worcestershire sauce**

Thaw frozen shrimp or drain canned shrimp. Rinse canned shrimp with cold water. Cut large shrimp in half. Fry bacon until crisp; drain on absorbent paper. Crumble bacon. Cook green pepper and onion in bacon drippings until tender. Add seasonings and shrimp; heat. Combine eggs, cream, Worcestershire sauce, and bacon. Add to shrimp mixture and cook until eggs are firm, stirring occasionally. Yield: 6 servings.

SHRIMP REMOULADE

- 3 **pounds fresh or frozen small or medium-sized shrimp**
- ¾ **cup mayonnaise**
- 2 **teaspoons dry mustard**
- 2 **stalks celery, minced**
- 6 **green onions, minced**
- 2 **drops hot pepper sauce**
- 1 **teaspoon salt**
- 1 **teaspoon paprika**
- 3 **sprigs parsley**

Boil and peel shrimp; chill. Mix mayonnaise, dry mustard, celery, onion, hot pepper sauce, salt, paprika, and parsley. Set aside and let blend for at least 3 hours. Pour over boiled shrimp and serve with thin, crisp party crackers. Yield: 8 servings.

SHRIMP RISOTTO

6 tablespoons butter or margarine, divided
1 pound fresh or frozen shrimp
½ teaspoon finely chopped garlic (optional)
　　or
½ small onion, chopped (optional)
½ cup sliced mushrooms (fresh or canned)
¼ cup chopped pimiento
2 tablespoons tomato paste
2 tablespoons all-purpose flour
1 cup heavy cream
1 teaspoon salt
　Few grains cayenne pepper
4 drops Worcestershire sauce
4 cups cooked rice

Melt 4 tablespoons butter in heavy pan over moderate heat. Add shrimp and stir 2 or 3 minutes. Remove shrimp from pan. Remove shells and cut shrimp in half lengthwise.

Melt remaining 2 tablespoons butter in a saucepan. Add chopped garlic or onion and sliced mushrooms. Stir over medium heat for 2 minutes. Add pimiento. Remove from heat and stir in tomato paste and flour. Add cream very gradually, stirring constantly. Add salt, cayenne pepper, and Worcestershire sauce. Place pan over moderate heat and stir until mixture comes to a boil. Add sliced shrimp and stir until reheated. Serve mixture with boiled rice. Yield: 8 servings.

GULF SHRIMP SALAD

¾ pound cooked, peeled, cleaned shrimp, fresh or frozen
　　or
3 (4½- or 5-ounce) cans shrimp
2 cups cooked rice
1 cup sliced celery
½ cup chopped parsley
¼ cup sliced ripe olives
½ cup mayonnaise or salad dressing
2 tablespoons French dressing
2 tablespoons freshly squeezed lemon juice
1 teaspoon curry powder
　Salad greens

Thaw shrimp if frozen or drain canned shrimp. Cover canned shrimp with ice water and let stand for 5 minutes; drain. Cut large shrimp in half. Combine rice, celery, parsely, olives, and shrimp. Combine mayonnaise, French dressing, lemon juice, and curry powder; mix thoroughly. Add mayonnaise mixture to shrimp mixture; toss lightly. Chill. Serve on salad greens.
Yield: 6 servings.

SEASHELL ROMETSCH

1½ pounds medium-to-large shrimp
2 tablespoons butter or margarine
1 medium onion, diced
⅛ pound ground beef
10 fresh mushrooms, sliced
1 clove garlic, minced
　Salt and pepper
2 tablespoons brown gravy*
3 tomatoes
½ head lettuce
　Green onions, diced
1 lemon

Sauté shrimp in 2 tablespoons butter. Add onion, ground beef, mushrooms, garlic, salt, and pepper. When almost done, add gravy. Let simmer until mixture glazes, about 10 minutes. Remove from heat. Peel tomatoes and slice vertically in strips. Slice lettuce in thin strips. Mix shrimp with tomato slices, diced green onions, and lettuce.

Toss lightly and squeeze fresh lemon juice over all. Serve in seashells or on small plates.
Yield: 6 to 8 servings.

*If you don't have brown gravy on hand, substitute gravy mix or a little beef bouillon and dash of Worcestershire sauce.

SHRIMP ROLLS

½ pound shrimp, fresh or frozen
1 cup shredded lettuce or other salad greens
　Few sprigs parsley or watercress, chopped
¼ cup chopped celery
¼ cup chopped cucumber
1 teaspoon chopped onion
　Mayonnaise
　Salt and pepper
3 or 4 frankfurter rolls
　Softened butter or margarine

Clean and cook shrimp. Reserve a few whole shrimp for garnishing and chop remaining shrimp. Toss shrimp with lettuce, parsley, celery, cucumber, and onion. Moisten with mayonnaise and season to taste with salt and pepper. Split frankfurter rolls, but do not cut all the way through. Spread rolls with softened butter and fill with shrimp salad. Garnish with the reserved whole shrimp. Yield: 3 or 4 servings.

SHRIMP MACARONI SALAD

¾ pound cooked, peeled, and cleaned shrimp,
  fresh or frozen
    or
3 (4½- or 5-ounce) cans shrimp
2 cups cooked shell macaroni
1 cup chopped raw cauliflower
1 cup sliced celery
¼ cup chopped parsley
¼ cup chopped sweet pickle
½ cup mayonnaise or salad dressing
3 tablespoons garlic French dressing
1 tablespoon freshly squeezed lemon juice
1 teaspoon grated onion
1 teaspoon celery seed
1 teaspoon salt
¼ teaspoon pepper
  Salad greens
1 hard-cooked egg, sliced

Thaw frozen shrimp or drain canned shrimp.
Rinse canned shrimp with cold water. Cut large
shrimp in half. Combine macaroni, cauliflower,
celery, parsley, pickle, and shrimp. Combine
mayonnaise, French dressing, lemon juice, onion,
and remaining seasonings; mix thoroughly. Add
mayonnaise mixture to shrimp mixture and toss
lightly; chill. Serve on salad greens. Garnish with
egg slices. Yield: 6 servings.

VEGETABLE-SHRIMP MACARONI SALAD

1 (8-ounce) package small shell macaroni
1 envelope unflavored gelatin
¼ cup water
1 (10-ounce) package frozen mixed vegetables
1 cup water
2½ teaspoons seasoned salt
2 tablespoons dried, crushed mint leaves
1½ teaspoons basil
1 (7-ounce) package frozen deveined shrimp,
  thawed and coarsely chopped
2 (8-ounce) cartons plain yogurt

Cook macaroni in boiling salted water 5 to 7
minutes or until tender, yet firm; drain. Soften
gelatin in ¼ cup water in large mixing bowl.
Combine vegetables, 1 cup water, salt, mint, and
basil in saucepan. Bring to boil, stir in shrimp, and
cook about 3 minutes, or until shrimp and
vegetables are tender. Stir shrimp mixture and
macaroni into gelatin. Refrigerate until mixture is
just cool. Thoroughly fold in yogurt. When ready
to serve, unmold and serve immediately.
Yield: 6 to 8 servings.

SHRIMP SALAD IN PINEAPPLE BASKET

1 large pineapple
2 cups cooked shrimp
½ cup slivered almonds
½ cup chopped celery
½ teaspoon salt
¼ teaspoon white pepper
½ teaspoon celery salt
2 tablespoons freshly squeezed lemon juice
½ cup salad dressing
  Crisp lettuce

Cut pineapple lengthwise into halves, leaving
green top on each half. Scoop pineapple from shell
and chop finely; drain thoroughly. Combine
pineapple, shrimp, almonds, celery, and
seasonings; add lemon juice and salad dressing.
Arrange in pineapple shells placed on a bed of
lettuce. Yield: 6 servings.

SHRIMP 'N' RICE SALAD

¼ cup salad oil
2 tablespoons cider vinegar
2 tablespoons chili sauce
1 tablespoon horseradish
½ teaspoon sugar
  Salt and pepper
2 cups cooked rice
½ pound cooked shrimp, cut in small pieces
2 tablespoons chopped parsley
2 tablespoons toasted almonds

Combine oil, vinegar, chili sauce, horseradish,
and sugar in saucepan. Heat and season with salt
and pepper to taste. Add rice and shrimp to mixed
seasonings and heat thoroughly, stirring
occasionally. Sprinkle with parsley and almonds
and serve at once. Yield: 4 servings.

SAUTEED SHRIMP PRONTO

1½ pounds raw shrimp
¼ cup butter or salad oil
1 (3-ounce) can sliced mushrooms
1 green pepper, chopped
½ cup chopped celery
½ teaspoon salt
¼ teaspoon pepper
  Dash hot pepper sauce

Shell and devein shrimp. Melt butter or oil in
frying pan. When hot add mushrooms, pepper,
celery, and seasonings except hot pepper sauce.
Add shrimp and cook, stirring until shrimp turn
pink and are tender. Add hot pepper sauce.
Yield: 6 servings.

SHRIMP SAVOY

12 cooked, cleaned shrimp
1 clove garlic, minced
1 tablespoon chopped chives
3 tablespoons butter or margarine
  Dash sherry
  Grated Parmesan cheese

Prepare shrimp. Sauté garlic and chives in butter until hot. Add shrimp. Turn several times in sauce. Add a good dash of sherry. Turn more to cover with sauce. Sprinkle with Parmesan cheese. Turn quickly. Serve hot. Yield: 2 servings.

SCAMPI

⅓ cup salad oil
1 pound shrimp, shelled and deveined
2 tablespoons chopped celery
½ tablespoon chopped green pepper
1 tablespoon chopped onion
1 clove garlic, minced
1 tablespoon chopped parsley
⅓ cup water
2 tablespoons freshly squeezed lemon juice
⅓ cup tomato paste
½ teaspoon salt
  Dash celery salt (optional)

Heat oil in skillet over medium heat; add shrimp, celery, green pepper, onion, and garlic. Sauté, turning often, until shrimp are just pink. Reduce heat; add remaining ingredients. Mix well. Simmer, stirring occasionally, for about 5 minutes or until shrimp are tender. Yield: 4 servings.

SPICED SHRIMP

1½ pounds shrimp, fresh or frozen
1 bunch celery tops
1 bunch parsley
1½ teaspoons crushed bay leaves
1½ teaspoons whole allspice
1½ teaspoons whole red peppers
1½ teaspoons whole peppercorns
¾ teaspoon whole cloves
1 cup vinegar
¼ cup salt
2 quarts boiling water

Wash shrimp but do not remove shells. Tie the celery, parsley, and spices in a piece of cheesecloth. Add vinegar, salt, and bag of seasonings to the water. Cover and simmer 45 minutes. Add shrimp, cover, and return to boiling point; simmer 5 minutes. Drain, peel, and devein. Serve with cocktail sauce. Yield: 6 servings.

STEAMED SHRIMP

Wash 2 pounds raw shrimp thoroughly several times.

Lift out of rinse water and place in heavy saucepan with tight-fitting lid. Add no more water than clings to shells. Place over heat with lid on and steam for 3 minutes.

Remove from pan and serve in shells with cocktail or lemon butter sauce. Yield: 4 servings.

SHRIMP SUPREME

3 pounds shrimp, fresh or frozen
2 (4-ounce) cans sliced mushrooms, drained
⅔ cup butter or margarine, melted
¼ cup chopped onion
2 tablespoons chili sauce
½ teaspoon garlic salt
  Dash hot pepper sauce
½ cup chopped parsley
2 tablespoons freshly squeezed lemon juice
1 teaspoon salt
  Dash Worcestershire sauce

Thaw shrimp if frozen. Peel shrimp and devein. Wash and drain on absorbent paper. Cut 6 squares of heavy-duty aluminum foil, 12 inches each. Divide shrimp into 6 portions. Place each portion of shrimp on a half of each square of foil. Top with mushrooms.

Combine the remaining ingredients to make a sauce; pour over shrimp, using approximately 3 tablespoons for each portion. Fold other half of foil over shrimp and seal edges by making double folds in the foil. Place packages of shrimp on a barbecue grill about 4 inches from moderately hot coals. Cook for 20 minutes, or until shrimp are tender. To serve, cut a big crisscross in the top of each package and fold back the foil. Yield: 6 servings.

SHRIMP WIGGLE

¾ pound cooked shrimp
¼ cup butter or margarine
¼ cup all-purpose flour
1 teaspoon salt
2 cups milk
1 cup cooked peas
  Patty shells, toast cups, or toast

Cut large shrimp in half. Melt butter; blend in flour and salt. Add milk gradually and cook until thick and smooth, stirring constantly. Stir in peas and shrimp; heat. Serve in patty shells, toast cups, or on toast. Yield: 6 servings.

Sauté onion in oil drained from tuna. When onion is tender, add rice, soup, cream, poultry seasoning, and pimiento; mix well. Gently mix in peas and tuna, which has been broken into chunks; pour into a casserole dish. Bake at 375° for about 40 minutes. Yield: 6 servings.

TUNA NOODLE CRISP

1 (5-ounce) package noodles, uncooked
¼ cup shortening
⅓ cup chopped onion
2 tablespoons chopped green pepper
1 (11-ounce) can cheese soup
½ cup milk
1 tablespoon chopped pimiento (optional)
1 teaspoon salt
⅛ teaspoon pepper
1 (7-ounce) can tuna
½ cup bread crumbs

Cook noodles in boiling salted water according to package directions; drain. Melt shortening in a large skillet; add onion and green pepper and sauté until tender. Stir in soup, milk, pimiento, salt, and pepper; bring to a boil. Add cooked noodles and tuna. Place mixture in a 1½- or 2-quart casserole dish. Sprinkle bread crumbs on top. Bake at 350° for 25 to 30 minutes.
Yield: 4 to 6 servings.
Note: To freeze, omit bread crumbs, cover tightly, and freeze. Thaw overnight. The next day add bread crumbs and bake as directed above.

TUNA-NOODLE CASSEROLE

8 ounces noodles
2 (10¾-ounce) cans cream of mushroom soup
2 cups milk
2 teaspoons salt
⅛ teaspoon pepper
2 tablespoons grated onion
2 cups frozen carrots and peas, partially cooked
¼ cup chopped pimiento
2 (7-ounce) cans flaked tuna

Cook noodles in boiling salted water. Drain and rinse. Combine soup, milk, salt, and pepper. Add onions, carrots and peas, pimiento, and tuna. Mix well. Combine with noodles. Pour into a greased 3-quart casserole dish. Bake at 375° for about 30 minutes. Yield: 8 to 10 servings.

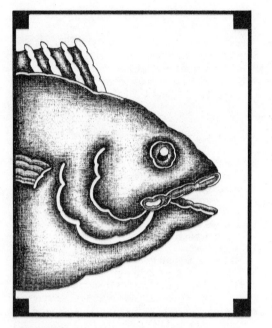

TUNA

Tuna is a familiar item in almost every American home. Canned tuna is available in three different styles of pack: fancy or solid, chunk-style, and flaked or grated. Tuna is most commonly packed in oil, although it may be packed in water.

Some of the speciality packs include a solid-meat tuna packed in olive oil and double the amount of salt, a "dietetic" pack in distilled water, a baby food, and a tuna paste.

Tuna has two outstanding recommendations. It contains a superior protein and it offers the busy homemaker a convenient food which may be easily prepared for a delicate dish.

TUNA-RICE CASSEROLE

1 medium onion, chopped
2 (6½- to 7-ounce) cans tuna, packed in oil
1½ cups cooked rice
1 (10¾-ounce) can cream of celery soup
1 cup light cream
1 teaspoon poultry seasoning
¼ cup diced pimiento
1 (17-ounce) can peas, drained

IMPERIAL TUNA

2 (7-ounce) cans chunk tuna
1 egg, beaten
1 hard-cooked egg, mashed
2 slices day-old white bread, finely crumbled
1 tablespoon minced pimiento
1 tablespoon finely minced green pepper
1 tablespoon finely minced onion
1 tablespoon minced parsley
4 teaspoons Worcestershire sauce
¼ cup mayonnaise
1 tablespoon butter or margarine
1 tablespoon milk or cream
  Paprika

Pick out large chunks of tuna, about ¼ of total amount, and place in the bottom of 6 well-greased custard cups. Combine eggs, bread crumbs, pimiento, green pepper, onion, parsley, Worcestershire sauce, half of the mayonnaise, butter, and remaining tuna; mix lightly and press over tuna chunks in cups. Carefully unmold and top with a blend of the remaining mayonnaise and milk. Sprinkle with paprika. Bake at 375° for 10 or 15 minutes, or until lightly brown.
Yield: 6 servings.

TUNA SALAD

1 (7-ounce) can tuna
¼ cup French dressing
3 hard-cooked eggs
2 small heads lettuce
½ cup chopped sweet pickles
1 teaspoon Worcestershire sauce

Break tuna in large pieces and marinate in dressing in refrigerator for 30 minutes. Chop eggs, shred lettuce (reserving outer leaves), and combine all ingredients. Serve in lettuce cups.
Yield: 6 servings.

MOLDED TUNA PATE WITH COGNAC

1 (4-ounce) can chopped mushrooms
1 envelope unflavored gelatin
1 tablespoon cognac
2 (7-ounce) cans tuna
¼ teaspoon hot pepper sauce
½ cup Green Goddess salad dressing
¼ cup parsley leaves
  Melba toast or crackers

Drain the liquid from the mushrooms into a blender. Sprinkle gelatin over the liquid and allow to soften. Heat ½ cup water to boiling and add to the blender. Blend at low speed until the gelatin is dissolved.

Add the mushrooms and remaining ingredients. Blend at high speed until thoroughly smooth. Pour into a 4-cup mold. Chill until firm.

Unmold and serve with Melba toast or crisp crackers. Yield: about 4 cups.

AVOCADO-TUNA CASSEROLE

2 medium avocados
1 cup chopped watercress or fresh spinach
1 small onion
2 (7-ounce) cans tuna
1 (10¾-ounce) can cream of chicken soup
½ cup milk
  Dash pepper
4 slices bacon
1 cup crushed potato chips

Peel and dice the avocados. Place in a greased 1½-quart casserole dish and top with watercress or spinach. Grate the onion over the watercress. Drain the tuna and flake slightly. Heat the soup with the milk; add pepper. Fry the bacon until crisp; drain on paper towel and crumble. Add the tuna and bacon to the hot soup. Pour over the avocado and sprinkle with potato chips. Bake at 450° for 10 minutes. Yield: 6 servings.

SUNDAY TUNA BRUNCH

1 (6½- or 7-ounce) can tuna, packed in oil
1 cup or stick pastry mix
½ cup chopped green onion
1½ tablespoons tuna oil
4 eggs, beaten
1½ cups half-and-half
2 tablespoons chopped parsley
½ teaspoon salt
  Dash pepper
¼ cup grated Swiss cheese
  Paprika

Drain tuna, reserving oil. Flake tuna. Prepare pastry mix as directed. Roll out pastry and line a 9-inch piepan. Bake pie shell at 450° for 7 to 10 minutes, or until light brown. Sauté onion in tuna oil until tender. Combine egg, half-and-half, parsley, salt, pepper, onion, and tuna. Pour into pie shell. Top with cheese; sprinkle with paprika. Bake at 350° for 35 to 45 minutes, or until knife inserted in the center comes out clean. Remove from oven and let stand for 10 minutes.
Yield: 6 servings.

TUNA BAKE

¼ cup milk
1 (7-ounce) can tuna
1 teaspoon Worcestershire sauce
2 teaspoons chopped onion
2 hard-cooked eggs, chopped
½ cup ripe olives, chopped
1 cup cooked rice
1 (10¾-ounce) can cream of mushroom soup
¼ teaspoon paprika
1 cup crushed potato chips

Combine first 8 ingredients and mix well. Spoon into a greased 2-quart casserole dish. Sprinkle top with paprika and spread crushed potato chips on top. Bake at 350° for 25 to 30 minutes. Yield: 6 to 8 servings.

SOUR CREAM-TUNA CASSEROLE

1 (10¾-ounce) can cream of mushroom soup
1 (10¾-ounce) can cream of celery soup
1 pint commercial sour cream
½ cup dry white wine (Sauterne)
½ teaspoon garlic salt
1 teaspoon onion salt
½ teaspoon freshly squeezed lemon juice
1 (7-ounce) can tuna
2 (5-ounce) packages egg noodles, cooked
　Shredded Cheddar cheese
　Bread crumbs

Combine first 7 ingredients in a 2-quart casserole dish. Stir well and add well-drained tuna. Add cooked egg noodles and mix thoroughly. Top with shredded cheese and bread crumbs. Bake at 400° for 15 minutes, or until cheese is melted and casserole is bubbling. Yield: 6 servings.

SOUTHERN TUNA CHOWDER

1 (6½- or 7-ounce) can tuna
2 chicken bouillon cubes
2 cups boiling water
¼ cup chopped onion
1 cup chopped celery
¼ cup butter or margarine, melted
3 tablespoons all-purpose flour
3 cups milk
1½ cups shredded cheese

Drain tuna. Break into large pieces. Dissolve bouillon cubes in boiling water. Sauté onion and celery in butter until tender. Blend in flour. Add milk and bouillon gradually to onion and celery mixture and cook until thick, stirring constantly. Add cheese and tuna; heat until cheese melts, stirring constantly. Yield: 6 servings.

SPECIAL TUNA CASSEROLE

1 (17-ounce) can green peas
1 (10¾-ounce) can cream of mushroom soup
¾ cup milk
1 (7-ounce) can tuna, drained and coarsely flaked
1¼ cups crushed potato chips

Drain peas. Empty soup into a greased 1-quart casserole dish. Add milk gradually and mix thoroughly. Add peas, tuna, and 1 cup potato chips. Mix well. Sprinkle top with remaining potato chips. Bake at 350° for 20 minutes. Yield: 4 servings.

TUNA-WATER CHESTNUT CASSEROLE

½ cup raw rice
1 (6-ounce) can water chestnuts, drained and sliced
2 stalks celery, diced
½ green pepper, diced
1 tablespoon instant minced onion
1 (10¾-ounce) can cream of mushroom soup
2 tablespoons freshly squeezed lemon juice
½ teaspoon salt
1 teaspoon Worcestershire sauce
1 teaspoon soy sauce
¼ teaspoon Ac'cent
1 (7-ounce) can tuna, drained
　Paprika

Cook rice according to package directions. Combine rice with all ingredients except tuna and paprika. Lightly stir in rice and flaked tuna. Turn into a shallow casserole dish. Sprinkle with paprika. Cover and bake at 350° for 30 minutes. Yield: 4 to 5 servings.

TUNA CORN CHOWDER

2 (6½- or 7-ounce) cans tuna
1 (10¾-ounce) can cream of potato soup
3 cups milk
1 tablespoon butter or margarine
1 tablespoon grated onion
1 small bay leaf
　Dash pepper
1 (8-ounce) can whole kernel corn
　Chopped parsley

Drain tuna and break into large pieces. Combine soup, milk, butter, onion, bay leaf, and pepper. Heat until well combined, stirring occasionally. Add corn and tuna; heat. Remove bay leaf. Garnish with parsley. Yield: 6 servings.

TUNA CHOWDER

    3   tablespoons chopped onion
    1½ cups diced potatoes
    ½   teaspoon salt
    1½ cups boiling water
    1   (10¾-ounce) can cream of mushroom soup
    1   cup milk
    1   (12-ounce) can whole kernel corn
        Dash pepper
    1   (7-ounce) can tuna, drained and flaked
    4   slices bacon
    2   tablespoons bacon drippings

Add onions, potatoes, and salt to boiling water; cook for 10 minutes or until potatoes are tender. Add soup, milk, corn, pepper, and tuna. Cook bacon. Add bacon drippings and more salt, if needed, to mixture; heat through. Crumble bacon and sprinkle over top of chowder before serving. Yield: 4 servings.

TUNA CROQUETTES

    ½   cup mayonnaise
    ¼   teaspoon salt
    ⅛   teaspoon pepper
    1   teaspoon Worcestershire sauce
    2   teaspoons water
    1   teaspoon grated onion
    2   tablespoons finely chopped green pepper
    1   cup cooked regular rice
    1½ cups drained flaked tuna
        Fine dry bread crumbs

Combine mayonnaise, seasonings, water, onion, and green pepper in bowl. Add rice and tuna. Mix with a fork; let stand for 5 minutes. Shape into croquettes and roll in bread crumbs. Place ½ inch apart on an ungreased cookie sheet lined with heavy brown paper. Bake at 450° for about 20 minutes, or until browned. Yield: 6 to 8 croquettes.

TUNA BISCUIT KERCHIEFS

Tuna Filling
    3   tablespoons butter or margarine
    ¾   cup chopped celery
    ⅓   cup diced onion
    ¼   cup all-purpose flour
    2   cups milk
    1   (7-ounce) can tuna, drained and flaked
    1½ cups cooked peas
    2   tablespoons diced pimiento
    ¼   teaspoon salt
    1½ cups shredded sharp cheese
        Biscuit Squares

Melt butter in saucepan; sauté celery and onion until tender. Blend in flour. Gradually add milk and cook until thickened, stirring constantly. Add tuna, peas, pimiento, and salt. Remove from heat and stir in cheese. Prepare Biscuit Squares.

Biscuit Squares
    3   cups all-purpose flour
    4   teaspoons baking powder
    1½ teaspoons salt
    ⅓   cup shortening
    ⅓   cup chopped parsley
    3   tablespoons chopped onion
    ¾   to 1 cup milk

Combine flour, baking powder, and salt in a bowl. Cut in shortening until mixture is crumbly. Mix in parsley and onion. Stir in enough milk to make a soft dough.

Turn out on a lightly floured board or pastry cloth and knead gently for 30 seconds. Divide dough in half. Roll each half into 6- x 20-inch rectangle; cut into three 6-inch squares and three 2-inch circles. Place each square in an individual casserole dish. Pour tuna filling into center of biscuit dough. Bring corners to meet in center. Place a circle over each center. Bake at 400° for about 20 minutes. Yield: 6 servings.

TUNA TETRAZZINI

    1   (5-ounce) package spaghetti, broken into
        2-inch pieces
    1   (10¾-ounce) can cream of celery soup
    ½   cup milk
    2   (7-ounce) cans tuna, drained and flaked
    1   (3-ounce) can sliced mushrooms, undrained
    ⅓   cup chopped onion
    ¼   cup sliced ripe olives
    1   (8-ounce) wedge sharp cheese, shredded

Cook spaghetti; drain. Stir in soup and milk. Add remaining ingredients, reserving ½ cup cheese for topping; mix lightly. Pour into 1½-quart casserole dish. Bake at 350° for 45 minutes. Sprinkle with remaining cheese; return to oven until cheese melts. Yield: 6 to 8 servings.

BASIC TUNA LOAF

    1   egg
    ¾   cup evaporated milk
    2   cups soft bread crumbs
    ½   teaspoon salt
    ½   teaspoon dry mustard
    ¼   teaspoon hot pepper sauce
    3   (6½- or 7-ounce) cans tuna

Combine egg, evaporated milk, bread crumbs, and seasonings in large mixing bowl. Beat until blended. Mix in tuna. Turn into a heavy-duty aluminum foil-lined 7½- x 3½- x 2½-inch loafpan. Bake at 350° for 45 minutes. Lift out of pan; remove foil. Yield: 6 servings.

SWEET-SOUR NEPTUNA

      3   tablespoons butter or margarine
      1   (20-ounce) can crushed pineapple
   1⅓   cups diced green pepper
      2   tablespoons cornstarch
      2   teaspoons soy sauce
      2   tablespoons freshly squeezed lemon juice
      ½   cup sugar
   1½   cups chicken broth or bouillon
      2   (6½- or 7-ounce) cans solid-pack tuna,
            drained
      ½   teaspoon salt
            Dash pepper
            Chinese noodles

Melt butter over low heat. Drain pineapple and reserve syrup. Add pineapple to butter and sauté for 5 minutes. Add ½ cup pineapple syrup and green pepper; cover and cook over low heat for 10 minutes.

Combine cornstarch and remaining pineapple syrup; blend well. Add cornstarch mixture, soy sauce, lemon juice, sugar, and broth to pineapple and green pepper mixture. Cook over medium heat until thickened, stirring constantly.

Break tuna into large pieces; add tuna, salt, and pepper to sauce and mix well. Heat to serving temperature. Serve over Chinese noodles. Yield: 6 servings.

TUNA ONE-DISH MEAL

      ⅓   cup butter or margarine
      3   tablespoons cornstarch
      ½   teaspoon salt
      ⅛   teaspoon pepper
      3   cups milk
      1   small onion, finely chopped
      2   (6½- or 7-ounce) cans tuna, drained and
            flaked
      1   (8-ounce) package elbow macaroni, cooked
            and drained
      1   (10-ounce) package frozen peas, thawed
      1   cup finely shredded Cheddar cheese
            Crushed potato chips

Melt butter in a saucepan over medium heat. Blend in cornstarch, salt, and pepper. Remove from heat and gradually stir in milk. Cook over medium heat, stirring constantly until mixture comes to boil and boils 1 minute. Remove from heat; stir in onion. Place tuna, macaroni, peas, and cheese in a greased 2-quart casserole dish. Stir in cornstarch mixture. Top with crushed potato chips. Bake at 350° for 20 to 25 minutes, or until bubbling hot. Yield: 6 to 8 servings.

TUNA-ONION PIE

   1½   cups salted cracker crumbs
      ½   cup butter or margarine
      3   onions
      2   tablespoons shortening
      1   cup milk
      3   eggs
      2   cups grated Swiss cheese
      1   pimiento, diced
      1   teaspoon salt
      ¼   teaspoon dry mustard
            Dash pepper
      1   (7-ounce) can tuna

Blend crumbs with melted butter; form a crust in a 9-inch pie plate; chill. Sauté thinly sliced onions in shortening until tender but not brown. Scald milk. Beat eggs until frothy; add cheese, pimiento, salt, mustard, pepper, and hot milk. Put half of onions in crust, cover with drained and flaked tuna and top with remaining onions. Pour egg and cheese mixture over all. Bake at 350° for 30 minutes. Yield: 6 servings.

SWISS TUNA-RICE PIE

      2   cups hot cooked rice
   1½   tablespoons butter or margarine
      1   egg, slightly beaten
      3   tablespoons chopped stuffed olives
      ¾   cup scalded milk
      2   eggs, slightly beaten
      4   tablespoons chopped onion
      ¼   teaspoon salt
            Dash pepper
      1   (7-ounce) can tuna
      1   cup shredded Swiss cheese

Combine rice and butter. Stir in 1 egg and chopped olives. Spread evenly over bottom and sides of a greased 9-inch piepan to make a shell. Gradually stir scalded milk into 2 eggs. Add onion, salt, pepper, and tuna. Pour into rice-lined piepan and sprinkle cheese over the top. Bake at 400° for 15 minutes; reduce heat to 300° and bake an additional 15 minutes. Yield: 6 servings.

TUNA LASAGNA

- ½ cup chopped onion
- 1 garlic clove, minced
- 1 tablespoon salad oil
- 2 (7-ounce) cans tuna, drained and flaked
- 1 (10¾-ounce) can cream of celery soup
- ½ cup milk
- ½ teaspoon oregano
- ¼ teaspoon pepper
- 1 (8-ounce) package lasagna noodles, cooked and drained
- 1 (6-ounce) package sliced Mozzarella cheese
- ½ pound pasteurized process cheese spread, thinly sliced
- ¼ cup grated Parmesan cheese

Sauté onion and garlic in oil until tender. Add tuna, soup, milk, oregano, and pepper. Layer noodles, Mozzarella cheese, tuna sauce, process cheese, and Parmesan cheese in 12- x 8-inch baking dish. Repeat layers. Bake at 350° for 30 minutes. Yield: 6 to 8 servings.

TUNA SUNSHINE PLATTER

- 1 (5-ounce) can chow mein noodles
- 1 (6½- or 7-ounce) can tuna
- 1 (10¾-ounce) can cream of mushroom soup
- 1 (8½-ounce) can peas, drained
- 2 hard-cooked eggs, sliced

Sprinkle noodles on platter. Combine tuna, soup, and drained peas in saucepan. Heat thoroughly. Pour over noodles. Garnish with hard-cooked eggs. Yield: 4 to 6 servings.

TUNA SLAW

- 2 (6½- or 7-ounce) cans tuna
- 2 cups shredded cabbage
- ½ cup mayonnaise or salad dressing
- ¼ cup chopped green pepper
- 2 tablespoons grated onion
- ½ teaspoon salt
  Dash pepper

Drain tuna. Break into large pieces. Combine all ingredients. Yield: 6 servings.

MANDALAY TUNA SALAD

- 1 (7-ounce) can tuna
- 1 teaspoon freshly squeezed lemon juice
- ⅓ cup mayonnaise
- 2 tablespoons light cream
- ¼ teaspoon salt
  Dash cayenne pepper
- 1 teaspoon prepared mustard
- 1 cup diced celery
- 1 cup diced, unpeeled apple
  Iceberg lettuce

Drain and flake tuna and sprinkle with lemon juice. Combine mayonnaise with light cream, salt, cayenne pepper, and mustard. Combine tuna, celery and apples with dressing. Serve on a bed of crisp lettuce. Yield: 4 to 6 servings.

TUNA CRUNCH SALAD

- 2 (7-ounce) cans tuna, drained and finely flaked
- ¼ cup chopped water chestnuts
- 1 tablespoon freshly squeezed lemon juice
- ½ cup mayonnaise or salad dressing
  Salt and pepper

Combine tuna and water chestnuts in a medium-size bowl; stir in lemon juice, then mayonnaise and salt and pepper to taste; chill. Yield: 2 cups.

GOLDEN GATE TUNA SALAD

- 2 (6½- or 7-ounce) cans tuna
- 1 clove garlic, peeled and quartered
- ½ cup salad or olive oil
- 1 cup ½-inch bread cubes
- 8 cups mixed salad greens
- ¼ teaspoon salt
  Dash pepper
- 1 egg, cooked 1 minute
- 1 tablespoon freshly squeezed lemon juice
- ¼ cup grated Parmesan cheese

Drain tuna; flake. Add garlic to oil and let stand at least 1 hour. Place bread cubes in a shallow baking pan and toast at 350°, stirring occasionally until bread is lightly browned on all sides. Remove garlic from oil. Gradually pour ¼ cup of garlic oil over toasted bread cubes, mixing lightly until all the oil is absorbed. Place salad greens, torn into bite-size pieces, in a large salad bowl. Sprinkle with salt and pepper. Pour remaining garlic oil over greens, toasting lightly. Break egg into salad. Add lemon juice and mix thoroughly. Add grated cheese, bread cubes, and tuna; toss lightly. Serve immediately. Yield: 6 servings.

TUNA STACK-UPS

18 slices bread
   Butter or margarine
 1 (7-ounce) can tuna, drained and flaked
 1 (3-ounce) can mushrooms, drained
 4 hard-cooked eggs, chopped
½ cup chopped ripe olives
¼ cup chopped green onions
¼ cup mayonnaise
 1 (10¾-ounce) can cream of chicken soup
 1 cup commercial sour cream

Trim bread; butter both sides. Combine tuna, mushrooms, eggs, olives, onions, and mayonnaise; spread on 12 bread slices. Assemble 6 triple-decker sandwiches, placing remaining buttered slices on top. Fasten corners with toothpicks. Toast on cookie sheet at 350° for 20 minutes, or until crisp and lightly browned. Mix soup and sour cream; heat thoroughly. Serve over sandwiches. Yield: 6 sandwiches.

TUNA-STUFFED TOMATOES

 2 (6½- or 7-ounce) cans tuna
 6 large tomatoes
 1 teaspoon salt
 1 cup shredded Cheddar cheese
 1 cup cooked rice
 1 egg, beaten
   Dash pepper
 1 tablespoon melted butter or margarine
¼ cup dry bread crumbs

Drain tuna; break into large pieces. Wash tomatoes. Remove stem ends and centers; sprinkle with salt. Combine cheese, rice, egg, pepper, and tuna. Place in tomatoes. Combine melted butter and crumbs; sprinkle over top of tomatoes. Place in a well-greased 10- x 6- x 2-inch baking dish. Bake at 350° for 30 to 40 minutes, or until tomatoes are tender. Yield: 6 servings.

TOSSED TUNA SALAD

 2 (6½- or 7-ounce) cans tuna
 1 clove garlic
 2 cups chopped raw spinach
 1 cup thinly sliced celery
 1 cup bean sprouts, drained
½ cup chopped cucumber
¼ cup chopped green onion
½ cup French dressing
   Tomato wedges

Drain tuna. Break into large pieces. Rub the inside of a salad bowl with the cut surface of a clove of garlic. Combine all ingredients except tomatoes; toss lightly. Garnish with tomato wedges. Yield: 6 servings.

SWEET-SOUR TUNA

2 (6½- or 7-ounce) cans tuna in salad oil
1 green pepper, cut in strips
1 cup diagonally cut celery
5 teaspoons cornstarch
1 (20-ounce) can pineapple chunks, drained and liquid reserved
2 tablespoons vinegar
2 teaspoons soy sauce
1 chicken-bouillon cube
   Hot cooked rice

Drain oil from 1 can of tuna into skillet; heat. Add green pepper and celery; sauté over high heat about 2 minutes, stirring constantly. Measure cornstarch into 2-cup measuring cup; gradually stir in pineapple syrup, vinegar, and soy sauce; add enough water to make 1½ cups.

Add this mixture to skillet with tuna, pineapple, and bouillon cube. Cook, stirring constantly, until sauce is clear and thickened and mixture is hot. Serve with hot cooked rice. Yield: 6 servings.

TUNA TEASERS

  1 cup all-purpose flour
1½ teaspoons baking powder
  1 teaspoon onion salt
 ½ teaspoon curry powder
    Dash cayenne pepper
 ¼ cup butter or margarine
 ½ cup milk
  1 (6½- or 7-ounce) can tuna, drained and flaked
  1 cup shredded American cheese
  1 tablespoon minced green pepper

Combine flour, baking powder, onion salt, curry powder, and cayenne pepper; cut in butter with pastry blender or fork until mixture resembles coarse meal. Add milk and stir until well blended. Add tuna, cheese, and green pepper; blend well.

Drop from teaspoon onto greased cookie sheet. Bake at 450° for 10 or 15 minutes, or until golden brown. Serve warm as an appetizer or with soup. Yield: 3 dozen.

MISCELLANEOUS FISH

In the past, certain varieties of fish could only be obtained at the market during certain times of the year. Today, fish can be purchased in almost any stage of preparation — fresh, frozen, cleaned, dressed, filleted, or even cut into steaks.

Whichever fish the cook prefers, she should select one with bright, clear, bulging eyes, reddish-pink gills free from slime or odor, and scales which are bright colored and adhere tightly to the skin. The flesh of the fish should be firm and elastic, springing back when pressed. Allow ⅓ to ½ pound of edible fish per person. If the fish is to be dressed at home, the larger amount should be selected.

The followng terms will be helpful in understanding what shape your fish is in:

Whole or round fish are those that are marketed in the same form as they come from the water. Before cooking they must be scaled and eviscerated (entrails removed). The head, tail, and fins may be removed if desired, and the fish split into serving-size portions.

Drawn fish are marketed with only the entrails removed.

Dressed or pan-dressed fish are scaled and eviscerated, usually with the head, tail, and fins removed.

Steaks are cross-sectional slices of the larger sizes of dressed fish.

Fillets are the sides of the fish, cut lengthwise away from the backbone. They are practically boneless and are ready to be cooked.

Of course, this cookbook is not only useful for the supermarket fisherman but also for the outdoor fisherman. Any kind of fish — trout, snapper, flounder, etc. — with a few fixin's can provide a mouth-watering dinner for your family.

SEAFOOD A LA KING

½ cup oysters
½ cup cooked shrimp
½ pound cooked conch meat
1 (10¾-ounce) can cream of celery soup
½ teaspoon salt
  Dash pepper
1 tablespoon chopped parsley
6 drops hot pepper sauce
1 tablespoon freshly squeezed lemon juice
  Toast points

Drain oysters; chop shrimp and conch meat. Heat soup with other ingredients. Add seafoods and heat again. Serve over toast points.
Yield: 6 servings.

FISH BAKE

1 pound fish fillets, fresh or frozen
1 teaspoon dehydrated onion flakes
3 cups tomato juice
1 teaspoon curry powder
½ teaspoon onion powder
1 teaspoon celery salt
¼ teaspoon garlic powder
1 bay leaf, broken
  Pinch of thyme
⅛ teaspoon pepper
2 teaspoons Worcestershire sauce

Thaw fish if frozen. Combine all ingredients, except fish, in a large covered saucepan. Heat well. Add fish, making sure it is covered with sauce. Simmer for about 20 minutes, or until fish flakes easily with a fork. Remove fish and serve.
Yield: about 2 servings.

BAKED CREAM FISH

2 pounds fish
2 tablespoons freshly squeezed lemon juice
1 (10¾-ounce) can cream of mushroom soup
½ cup milk
1 tablespoon dry mustard
½ cup bread crumbs
1 tablespoon minced parsley
¼ teaspoon paprika

Cut fish in serving-size pieces, no more than ½ inch thick. Place in a greased baking dish and sprinkle with lemon juice. Combine soup, milk, and mustard; pour over fish. Top with crumbs; sprinkle with parsley and paprika. Bake at 350° for 35 minutes, or until done. Yield: 6 servings.

SEAFOOD GUMBO

- 1 **pound okra, sliced**
- 4 **tablespoons shortening**
- 2 **tablespoons all-purpose flour**
- 1 **onion, chopped**
- 1 **bunch green onions, chopped**
- ½ **cup chopped celery**
- 1 **(1-pound) can tomatoes**
- 2 **sprigs parsley, chopped**
- 1 **bay leaf**
- 1 **sprig thyme**
- 2 **quarts water**
  Salt and pepper
- 1 **pound headless, raw shrimp**
- ½ **pound crabmeat, or 1 dozen crabs**
- 1 **teaspoon filé (optional)**

Fry okra in 2 tablespoons shortening until it ceases to "rope". Make roux in a heavy skillet by cooking shortening and flour until dark brown. Add onions and celery; cook until soft, about 5 minutes. Add okra. Stir in tomatoes, parsley, bay leaf, thyme, and water. Simmer for 30 minutes. Season. Add peeled, deveined, and washed shrimp and crabmeat or crabs and simmer for 30 minutes longer. Remove from heat. If desired, stir in filé just before serving (never cook filé). Gumbo is better if cooked early in the morning and refrigerated for several hours. Reheat and serve with cooked rice. Yield: 6 servings.

Note: If crab is used, scald live hard-shelled crabs and clean, removing the spongy substance and the "sand bag" on the under part. Break off and crack the claws, and cut the body in half.

BAKED STUFFED FISH

- ½ **cup butter or margarine, divided**
- ⅓ **cup chopped onion**
- ¼ **cup chopped parsley**
- ½ **cup finely chopped celery**
- 6 **cups soft bread cubes**
- 1¾ **teaspoons salt, divided**
- ⅛ **teaspoon pepper**
- 1 **(3- to 4-pound) fish, dressed for stuffing**
  Lemon slices
  Parsley
  Caper Sauce

Melt ⅓ cup butter; sauté onion, chopped parsley, and celery in butter until onion is tender.

Add bread cubes, ¼ teaspoon salt, and pepper; stir to coat bread cubes. Brown bread cubes lightly, stirring constantly.

Sprinkle remaining salt over inside and outside of fish. Stuff fish loosely with bread mixture; close opening with skewers to hold dressing in place. Place in greased shallow baking dish or oven-proof platter. Brush fish with remaining butter. Bake at 350° for 45 to 60 minutes, or until fish flakes easily with a fork. Baste often with pan drippings during baking. Garnish with lemon slices and parsley. Serve with Caper Sauce. Yield: 6 servings.

Caper Sauce

- 2 **tablespoons butter or margarine**
- ¼ **cup chopped onion**
- 2 **tablespoons all-purpose flour**
- ½ **teaspoon salt**
- 1½ **cups milk**
- 2 **tablespoons freshly squeezed lemon juice**
- 2 **tablespoons drained capers**
- 1 **tablespoon chopped parsley**

Melt butter and sauté onion until tender. Blend in flour and salt; mix well. Add milk, stirring constantly. Cook until sauce is smooth and has thickened. Stir in lemon juice, capers, and parsley. Serve with Baked Stuffed Fish. Yield: 1½ cups.

BAKED STUFFED BASS

- 1 **3- to 4-pound bass, cleaned**
  Salt and pepper to taste
- ¼ **cup butter or margarine**
- ¼ **cup chopped onion**
- ½ **cup chopped celery**
- 4 **cups dry bread crumbs**
- 1 **egg, beaten (optional)**
- ¼ **teaspoon thyme**
- ½ **teaspoon sage (optional)**
- 1 **teaspoon salt**
- ⅛ **teaspoon pepper**
  Melted butter or bacon slices

Dry fish and sprinkle inside with salt and pepper. Place fish on a well-greased, bake-and-serve platter or baking pan. Melt butter in a skillet and sauté the onion and celery in it until they are tender. Add to bread crumbs, along with egg and the seasonings. Mix thoroughly, and add 2 tablespoons water if dressing seems dry.

Stuff fish loosely with dressing. Brush with melted butter, or cover with slices of bacon held in place with toothpicks. Bake at 350° for 45 minutes to 1 hour, or until fish flakes easily with a fork. Yield: 6 servings.

BARBECUED BASS

2 **pounds bass fillets**
½ **cup salad oil**
½ **cup sesame seed**
⅓ **cup freshly squeezed lemon juice**
⅓ **cup cognac**
3 **tablespoons soy sauce**
1 **teaspoon salt**
1 **clove garlic, crushed**

Place fillets in a single layer in a shallow bowl.
Combine other ingredients and pour over fish.
Let stand for 30 minutes, turning once. Remove
fish, and reserve sauce for basting. Place fish on
well-greased wire grills. Cook for 8 minutes on
barbecue grill about 4 inches from moderately hot
coals. Baste while fish is cooking. Turn and
cook for about 7 minutes on other side. Serve
remaining sauce with fish. Yield: 6 servings.

BARBECUED STRIPED BASS STEAKS

2 **pounds striped bass steaks or other fish steaks,**
   fresh or frozen
½ **cup melted shortening**
½ **cup sesame seed**
⅓ **cup freshly squeezed lemon juice**
⅓ **cup cognac**
3 **tablespoons soy sauce**
1 **teaspoon salt**
1 **clove garlic, crushed**

Thaw steaks if frozen. Place steaks in a single
layer in a shallow baking pan. Combine remaining
ingredients. Pour sauce over fish and let stand for
30 minutes, turning once. Remove fish, reserving
sauce for basting. Place fish in well-greased,
hinged wire grills. Cook on a barbecue grill about
4 inches from moderately hot coals for 8
minutes. Baste with remaining sauce. Turn and
cook for 7 to 10 minutes longer, or until fish
flakes easily with a fork and sesame seeds have
browned. Serve any remaining sauce with
fish. Yield: 6 servings.

BROILED BASS

4 **pounds bass**
2 **teaspoons salt**
¼ **teaspoon pepper**
½ **cup butter or margarine**
   Juice of one-half lemon

Use whole pan-dressed fish or fillets. Sprinkle
with salt and pepper. Place on heavy-duty
aluminum foil or greased broiler pan, skin side up.

Brush with butter or with half butter and half
freshly squeezed lemon juice. Place 2 to 3 inches
from source of heat and broil 5 to 7 minutes,
or until lightly browned. Baste with butter; then
turn carefully. Baste again and broil 5 to 7
minutes, or until fish flakes easily with a
fork. Yield: 8 servings.

Note: An easy trick for turning whole fish:
Cut 2 pieces of paper the size of the whole fish;
grease both well. In broiler pan lay fish on one
piece of paper. When fish is ready to be turned,
place other greased paper on top, turn fish,
and remove first paper.

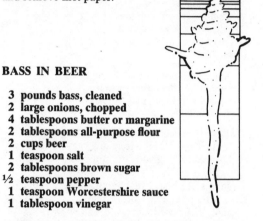

BASS IN BEER

3 **pounds bass, cleaned**
2 **large onions, chopped**
4 **tablespoons butter or margarine**
2 **tablespoons all-purpose flour**
2 **cups beer**
1 **teaspoon salt**
2 **tablespoons brown sugar**
½ **teaspoon pepper**
1 **teaspoon Worcestershire sauce**
1 **tablespoon vinegar**

Cut fish in 3-inch slices. Brown onion in butter.
Add flour and cook for about 2 minutes.
Add beer and all other ingredients except vinegar
and fish. Boil until sauce has thickness of thin
cream. Add fish and cook until fish flakes easily.
Add vinegar and cook an additional 2 minutes.
Fish may be served in sauce, or sauce may
be strained and served separately.
Yield: 4 to 6 servings.

BASS WITH OYSTER STUFFING

2 **(3- to 4-pound) bass, split and boned**
   Oyster Stuffing
¼ **cup melted butter or margarine**
   Salt and pepper to taste

Grease shallow pan, or line with heavy-duty
aluminum foil. Place 2 halves of fish, skin side
down, in pan. Spread with Oyster Stuffing; place
other halves, skin side up, on stuffing. Fasten
with skewers. Brush with melted butter; sprinkle
with salt and pepper. Bake at 350° for about
1 hour. Brush occasionally with butter.
Yield: 6 servings.

Oyster Stuffing

- **1 cup oysters, chopped**
- **3 cups dry bread cubes**
- **2 teaspoons salt**
- **⅛ teaspoon pepper**
- **⅛ teaspoon sage**
- **3 tablespoons butter or margarine**
- **1 small onion, minced**
- **2 tablespoons minced parsley**
- **½ cup minced celery**

Place oysters in a skillet; sauté about 5 minutes; drain. Combine bread cubes, salt, pepper, sage, and oysters. Melt butter in another skillet; add onion, parsley, and celery; sauté until tender. Add to oyster mixture.

SAUCY BROILED FISH

- **6 skinned, pan-dressed fish**
- **1 cup salad oil**
- **¼ cup chopped parsley**
- **2 tablespoons catsup**
- **2 tablespoons wine vinegar**
- **2 cloves garlic, finely chopped**
- **2 teaspoons basil**
- **1 teaspoon salt**
- **¼ teaspoon pepper**

Place fish in a single layer in a shallow baking dish. Combine remaining ingredients. Pour sauce over fish and marinate for 30 minutes, turning once. Remove fish, reserving sauce for basting. Place fish on a well-greased broiler pan. Brush with sauce. Broil about 3 inches from heat for 5 to 7 minutes, or until lightly browned, basting twice. Turn carefully and brush other side with sauce. Broil 5 to 7 minutes longer, basting occasionally, or until fish is brown and flakes easily with a fork. Yield: 6 servings.

BROILED FISH SUPREME

- **6 or 8 fish fillets (flounder, sole, or other fish)**
- **¼ cup melted shortening or butter**
- **½ cup mayonnaise**
- **2 eggs yolks**
- **1 tablespoon chopped parsley**
- **1 tablespoon chopped pimiento**
- **1 teaspoon chopped onion**
  Dash cayenne pepper
- **2 egg whites**

Brush fish fillets with the shortening. Broil lightly for 2 or 3 minutes. Turn, brush other side with shortening, and broil another 2 or 3 minutes. Fillets will puff and brown lightly.

Beat the mayonnaise; add egg yolks and beat well. Add parsley, pimiento, onion, and pepper; mix well. Beat egg whites until stiff and gently fold into the mixture. Spread over broiled fish and brown lightly. The sauce mixture will puff up and make a brown cover for fish. Watch carefully. Yield: 4 to 6 servings.

TANGY SEAFOOD CANAPES

- **1 cup flaked canned fish, crabmeat, lobster meat, or shrimp**
- **3 tablespoons mayonnaise or salad dressing**
- **1 tablespoon finely chopped celery**
- **½ cup butter or margarine**
- **3 tablespoons horseradish**
- **32 toast points**
  Chopped parsley

Drain canned fish or remove any shell or cartilage from shellfish. Combine mayonnaise, celery, and fish; blend into a paste. Combine butter and horseradish. Spread horseradish butter on toast points. Top with fish mixture. Garnish with parsley sprinkled over the top. Yield: 32 canapés.

SURFER'S SEAFOOD CASSEROLE

- **½ pound fresh crabmeat**
- **½ pound cooked shrimp**
- **1 cup mayonnaise**
- **1⅓ cups chopped celery**
- **½ cup chopped onion**
- **½ cup chopped green pepper**
- **½ teaspoon salt**
- **1 teaspoon Worcestershire sauce**
- **1 cup crushed potato chips**
  Paprika

Mix all ingredients except potato chips and paprika. Put mixture into a greased 1½-quart shallow casserole dish. Cover with crushed potato chips. Sprinkle with paprika. Bake at 350° for 30 to 40 minutes. Yield: 6 servings.

SEAFOOD EN CASSEROLE

    1 cup dry white wine
    1 small onion, sliced
    ½ bay leaf
    6 sprigs parsley
    1 teaspoon salt
    1 (8-ounce) package frozen scallops
    2 teaspoons freshly squeezed lemon juice
    1 (8-ounce) can mushroom slices
    ¼ cup butter or margarine
    ¼ cup all-purpose flour
    1 cup cooked crab, flaked
    1 cup cooked, diced lobster
    1 cup cooked shrimp
       Dash pepper
    6 tablespoons grated Swiss cheese
    ½ cup bread crumbs

Combine first 5 ingredients, and bring to a boil; add thawed sliced scallops; simmer 10 minutes. Discard onion, bay leaf, and parsley. Drain scallops; combine liquid with lemon juice and mushroom liquid; add water if necessary to make 2 cups. Melt butter, blend in flour, add liquid; cook over medium heat, stirring constantly until thickened. Cook over lowest heat 10 minutes. Add seafood, pepper, and mushrooms to sauce; heat through. Turn into a 2-quart casserole dish or individual shells. Top with cheese and crumbs; brown lightly under broiler. Yield: 8 servings.

CAJUN CATFISH

    6 skinned, pan-dressed catfish or other fish,
       fresh or frozen
    ½ cup tomato sauce
    2 (¾-ounce) packages cheese-garlic salad
       dressing mix
    2 tablespoons salad oil
    2 tablespoons chopped parsley
    2 tablespoons grated Parmesan cheese

Thaw fish if frozen. Clean, wash, and dry fish. Combine remaining ingredients except cheese. Brush fish inside and out with sauce. Place in a well-greased 13- x 9- x 2-inch baking dish. Brush with remaining sauce and sprinkle with cheese. Let stand for 30 minutes. Bake at 350° for 25 to 35 minutes, or until fish flakes easily with a fork. Turn oven control to broil. Place fish about 3 inches from source of heat and broil for 1 to 2 minutes, or until crisp and lightly browned. Yield: 6 servings.

CATFISH CAPER

    2 pounds skinned catfish fillets, fresh or frozen
    ½ cup salad oil
    ⅓ cup freshly squeezed lemon juice
    ¼ cup chopped onion
    2 tablespoons capers and juice
    2 tablespoons catsup
    1 tablespoon salt
    2 teaspoons Worcestershire sauce
    2 teaspoons sugar
    4 bay leaves, crushed
    2 cloves garlic, finely chopped
    ¼ teaspoon pepper
       Paprika

Thaw fillets if frozen. Place in a single layer in a shallow baking dish. Combine remaining ingredients except paprika. Pour sauce over fillets and let stand for 30 minutes, turning once. Remove fillets, reserving sauce for basting. Place fillets in well-greased, hinged wire grills. Sprinkle with paprika. Cook about 4 inches from moderately hot coals for 8 minutes. Baste with sauce and sprinkle with paprika. Turn and cook 7 to 10 minutes longer, or until fish flakes easily with a fork. Yield: 6 servings.

BAYOU CATFISH

    6 skinned, pan-dressed catfish or other fish,
       fresh or frozen
    1 cup dry white wine
    ½ cup melted butter or margarine
    1 (4-ounce) can mushroom stems and pieces,
       drained
    ¼ cup chopped green onions
    2 tablespoons freshly squeezed lemon juice
    2 tablespoons chopped parsley
    2 teaspoons salt
    ¼ teaspoon crushed bay leaves
    ¼ teaspoon pepper
    ¼ teaspoon thyme

Thaw fish if frozen. Clean, wash, and dry fish. Cut 6 (18-inch) squares of heavy-duty aluminum foil. Grease lightly. Place each fish on one half of each square of foil. Combine remaining ingredients. Pour sauce over fish, using approximately ⅓ cup sauce for each fish. Fold other half of foil over fish and seal edges by making double folds in the foil. Place packages of fish on a barbecue grill about 6 inches from moderately hot coals. Cook for 20 to 25 minutes, or until fish flakes easily with a fork. To serve, cut a big crisscross in the top of each package and fold the foil back. Yield: 6 servings.

MEMPHIS BAKED CATFISH

⅓ cup slivered almonds
1½ pounds catfish fillets
2 tablespoons freshly squeezed lemon juice
1 tablespoon barbecue sauce
1 tablespoon Worcestershire sauce
½ teaspoon salt
 Dash pepper

Place almonds in a shallow pan; toast at 300°
for 20 minutes. Remove almonds and set
oven temperature at 325°.
 Score fish with cuts from 1 to 1½ inches apart.
Combine lemon juice, sauces, and seasonings;
rub mixture into the fish. Place fillets in a lightly
greased shallow pan; sprinkle with toasted
almonds. Bake for 1½ hours. Serve at once.
Yield: 4 servings.

SOUTHERN CATFISH STEW

1 pound skinned catfish fillets or other fish
 fillets, fresh or frozen
½ cup chopped bacon
1 cup chopped onion
1 (28-ounce) can tomatoes
2 cups diced potatoes
1 cup boiling water
¼ cup catsup
2 tablespoons Worcestershire sauce
1 teaspoon salt
¼ teaspoon pepper
¼ teaspoon thyme

Thaw fillets if frozen. Cut into 1-inch pieces.
Fry bacon until crisp and browned. Add onion and
cook until tender. Add tomatoes, potatoes, water,
catsup, and seasonings. Cover and simmer for
30 minutes. Add fish. Cover and simmer about 15
minutes longer, or until potatoes are tender.
Yield: 6 servings.

Conserve Charcoal

Line the firebox with heavy-duty aluminum foil
to catch drippings and keep the grill clean.
 Place a layer of tiny stones in the firebox.
This is an aid to ventilation and prevents the coals
from burning out.
 Don't waste charcoal. When all cooking has
been completed, either lower hood to put out the
fire, or extinguish it with water.
 Be sure to dry charcoal before using again.
If fire was on the ground, extinguish with
dirt and water.

CATFISH STEW

½ pound fatback bacon
5 pounds catfish
3 medium onions, sliced
4 medium potatoes, sliced
 Salt and pepper to taste
 Milk (optional)

Place thin slices of bacon in a Dutch oven
over low heat, frying out all the fat possible. Pour
half of this into a container to be used later in
cooking the stew. To the remaining fat add sliced
onions and cook until slightly brown. Add a
layer of fish to the onion and fat, then a layer of
sliced potatoes, then another layer of fish,
alternating fish and potatoes until both are used
up. On top of the final layer add the rest of the
fat so it will penetrate all layers of the stew.
Add salt and pepper to taste. Cover and let cook
on low heat until the fish is ready to fall from
the bones. Do not stir too often as stirring
tends to break up the fish.
 For a generous amount of gravy, add one cup
milk and cook for 3 minutes. Serve hot.
Yield: 8 to 10 servings.

FISH CHOWDER

1 pound fish fillets
2 tablespoons chopped bacon
½ cup chopped onions
2 cups hot water
1 cup diced potatoes
2 cups milk or half-and-half
¾ teaspoon salt
 Dash pepper
 Chopped parsley

Cut fillets in 1-inch cubes. Fry bacon until crisp
and browned. Add onions and brown slightly.
Add water and potatoes and cook 10 minutes, or
until potatoes are partially tender. Add fish,
and cook until it can be flaked easily with a fork.
Add milk and seasonings; heat. Serve immediately
with chopped parsley sprinkled over the top.
Yield: 6 servings.

CAPTAIN "BO'S" FISH CHOWDER

2 cups diced potatoes
1 large green pepper, finely chopped
1 large onion, finely chopped
1 large clove garlic, minced
½ cup chopped celery
1 cup salad oil
1 (16-ounce) can tomatoes
1 (6-ounce) can tomato paste
2 cups water
2 bay leaves
2 tablespoons Worcestershire sauce
  Salt and pepper to taste
3 large carrots, cleaned and sliced
3 pounds fillet of flounder (or fish of your choice)
2 cups shrimp
1 small lemon, sliced
2 tablespoons chopped parsley
3 hard-cooked eggs, sliced

Brown potatoes, green pepper, onion, garlic, and celery in salad oil. Add tomatoes, tomato paste, water, bay leaves, Worcestershire sauce, salt, pepper, and carrots. Simmer for at least 30 minutes. Add fish, shrimp, lemon, eggs, and parsley and cook an additional 15 minutes, or until fish and shrimp are done. Yield: 8 to 10 servings.

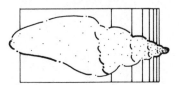

SEAFOOD A LA FRANCAISE

¾ pound shrimp, cooked and peeled
¾ pound lump crabmeat
6 shallots or green onions, chopped
12 mushroom buttons, finely chopped
¼ pound butter or margarine
4 tablespoons all-purpose flour
1 cup heavy cream
⅓ cup water
2 egg yolks
1½ cups dry white wine
  Juice of 1 lemon
  Salt and pepper to taste
2 dashes hot pepper sauce
  Grated Parmesan cheese
  Fine, dry bread crumbs

Sauté shrimp, crabmeat, shallots, and mushrooms lightly in hot melted butter (be careful not to burn butter). Sprinkle flour into mixture and toss gently so as not to break up crabmeat (do not let flour brown).

Combine cream and water; heat, and add to seafood mixture. Stir gently until mixture thickens. Beat egg yolks and add to mixture; stir in thoroughly, but gently. Add white wine and juice of lemon. Add salt and pepper to taste; add hot pepper sauce. Let simmer until thick, stirring constantly. Remove from heat, and let cool slightly.

Place mixture in lightly greased individual casserole dishes or ungreased coquille shells. Sprinkle dishes with grated Parmesan cheese and bread crumbs and glaze under broiler or in oven until brown. Yield: 6 servings.

SEAFOOD CROQUETTES

3 tablespoons cornstarch
1 cup milk
¾ teaspoon salt
1 tablespoon freshly squeezed lemon juce
  Dash pepper
2 teaspoons chopped parsley
1 teaspoon chopped celery
1 teaspoon finely chopped green onion top
1 (1-pound) can salmon
  Bread crumbs
1 egg, well beaten
  Hot shortening

Combine cornstarch and ¼ cup milk in a saucepan and heat, stirring. Let cool; then add the the rest of the milk and salt. Cook, stirring constantly, until thick. Add lemon juice, pepper, parsley, celery, onion, and salmon. Mix well and form into cone-shaped croquettes. Roll croquettes in crumbs, then in beaten egg, and again in crumbs. Fry in deep hot shortening until brown. Drain on absorbent paper. Yield: 6 servings.

PUFFY FILLETS AND ASPARAGUS

1½ pounds fish fillets
1 tablespoon freshly squeezed lime juice
  Salt and pepper
1 (14½-ounce) can asparagus, drained
1 cup milk
2 cups shredded Cheddar cheese

Arrange fish fillets in a greased shallow pan; spoon lime juice over fish and sprinkle with salt and pepper. Broil 3 inches from heat for 10 minutes. Arrange asparagus over fish. Heat milk in top of double boiler; add shredded cheese and stir until cheese has melted. Spoon over fish and asparagus; return to oven and broil on lowest rack for about 10 minutes. Yield: 6 servings.

ROLLED FILLETS WITH HERBS

1½ pounds fish fillets
1 teaspoon salt
   Dash pepper
   Dried marjoram
1½ cups milk
2 tablespoons butter or margarine
2 tablespoons all-purpose flour
¾ cup shredded Cheddar cheese
2 tablespoons sherry

Sprinkle fillets with salt, pepper, and marjoram.
Roll and secure with toothpicks. Place in a
shallow baking dish and add milk. Bake at 350°
for 30 minutes. Melt butter and add flour.
When fish is baked, pour off the milk into the flour
mixture, and cook until thick. Add cheese and
stir until melted; add sherry. Yield: 6 servings.

FLOUNDER SUPREME

2 pounds flounder fillets or other thin fish fillets,
   fresh or frozen
1 teaspoon salt
   Dash pepper
1 (4-ounce) can sliced mushrooms
2 tablespoons butter or margarine
½ cup chopped onion
¼ cup mushroom liquid
¼ cup dry white wine
1 tablespoon chopped parsley
1 tablespoon all-purpose flour
¾ cup half-and-half
   Dash white pepper
¼ cup shredded Cheddar cheese

Thaw fillets if frozen and skin. Sprinkle both
sides with salt and pepper. Roll fillets and secure
with picks. Drain mushrooms, reserving liquid.
Melt butter in a large frying pan. Add mushrooms
and onion and cook until tender. Place fish
rolls in pan. Add mushroom liquid and wine.
Sprinkle parsley over fish. Cover and bring to the
boiling point. Reduce heat and simmer for 8 to
10 minutes, or until fish flakes easily with a fork.
Remove fish to an oven glass or metal serving
platter; keep warm. Combine flour and
half-and-half to make a thin paste. Add gradually
to hot liquid and cook until thick, stirring
constantly. Add pepper. Pour over fish and
sprinkle with cheese. Broil about 5 inches from
source of heat for 2 to 3 minutes, or until cheese
melts and is lightly browned. Yield: 6 servings.

BROILED FLOUNDER

2 to 2½ pounds flounder fillets
   Salt and pepper
½ cup mayonnaise
¼ cup pickle relish
2 tablespoons chopped parsley
1 tablespoon freshly squeezed lemon juice
¼ teaspoon salt
   Dash cayenne pepper
2 egg whites

Wipe fillets with damp cloth, and if necessary
cut into serving-size pieces. Sprinkle with salt
and pepper; arrange on a lightly greased
shallow baking pan.
Stir together all other ingredients except egg
whites. Then fold in egg whites which have been
beaten until stiff but not dry. Broil fish 2 inches
from source of heat for 6 to 10 minutes, or
until nearly cooked through. Spread sauce in an
even layer over top of fish; broil 3 to 5 minutes
longer, or until sauce is puffy and lightly browned.
Serve at once with broiled tomato halves.
Yield: 6 servings.

FLOUNDER KIEV

2 pounds flounder fillets, fresh or frozen
½ cup soft butter or margarine
2 tablespoons chopped parsley
1 tablespoon freshly squeezed lemon juice
¾ teaspoon Worcestershire sauce
¼ teaspoon hot pepper sauce
1 clove garlic, finely chopped
½ teaspoon salt
   Dash pepper
½ cup all-purpose flour
2 eggs, beaten
2 tablespoons water
   Bread crumbs

Thaw fillets if frozen. Combine butter, parsley,
lemon juice, Worcestershire sauce, hot pepper
sauce, and garlic. Place butter mixture on waxed
paper and form into a roll. Chill until hard.
Skin fillets and divide into 12 strips about 6 x 2
inches. Sprinkle fish with salt and pepper.
Cut butter roll into 12 pieces. Place a piece of
butter at one end of each strip of fish. Fasten
with toothpicks. Roll fish in flour; dip in beaten
eggs, to which water has been added, and roll
in crumbs. Chill for 1 hour. Fry in deep fat at
375° for 2 to 3 minutes, or until golden brown and
fish flakes easily with a fork. Drain on absorbent
paper. Remove toothpicks before serving.
Yield: 6 servings.

FLOUNDER WITH CRABMEAT STUFFING

6 pan-dressed flounder (¾-pound each),
  fresh or frozen
1 pound crabmeat, fresh or frozen
       or
2 (6½-ounce) cans crabmeat
½ cup chopped onion
⅓ cup chopped celery
⅓ cup chopped green pepper
2 cloves garlic, finely chopped
⅓ cup salad oil
2 cups soft bread crumbs
3 eggs, beaten
1 tablespoon chopped parsley
2 teaspoons salt
½ teaspoon pepper
¾ cup salad oil
⅓ cup freshly squeezed lemon juice
2 teaspoons salt
  Paprika

Thaw fish if frozen. Clean, wash, and dry fish.
To make a pocket for the stuffing lay the fish
flat on a cutting board, light side down. With a
sharp knife cut down the center of the fish to the
backbone from the tail to about one inch from
the other end. Turn the knife flat and cut the flesh
along both sides of the backbone to the tail,
allowing the knife to run over the rib bones.

Thaw frozen crabmeat or drain canned
crabmeat. Remove any shell or cartilage. Cook
onion, celery, green pepper, and garlic in ⅓ cup
salad oil until tender. Combine bread crumbs,
eggs, parsley, salt, pepper, cooked vegetables, and
crabmeat; mix well. Stuff each fish loosely with
approximately ⅔ cup stuffing. Combine ¾ cup
oil, lemon juice, and salt. Cut 6 squares of
heavy-duty aluminum foil, 18 inches each. Grease
lightly. Place 2 tablespoons lemon sauce on one
half of each square of foil. Place fish in sauce. Top
each fish with 1 tablespoon lemon sauce.
Sprinkle with paprika. Fold other half of foil over
fish and seal edges by making double folds in
the foil. Place packages of fish on a barbecue grill
about 6 inches from moderately hot coals.
Cook for 25 to 30 minutes, or until fish flakes
easily with a fork. To serve, cut a big crisscross in
the top of each package and fold the foil back.
Yield: 6 servings.

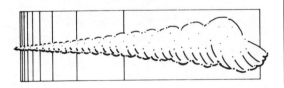

BAKED STUFFED FLOUNDER

½ cup chopped celery
½ cup chopped green onions, including tops
1 clove garlic, minced
½ cup butter or margarine, divided
1½ cups moistened bread cubes
½ pound boiled shrimp, chopped
½ pound crabmeat
2 tablespoons chopped parsley
1 egg, slightly beaten
  Salt, black pepper, and cayenne pepper
4 medium-size flounder

Sauté celery, onion, and garlic in ¼ cup butter
over low heat. Add bread, shrimp, crabmeat,
parsley, and egg; mix well. Season with salt, black
pepper, and cayenne pepper. Split thick side of
flounder, lengthwise and crosswise, and loosen
meat from bone of fish to form a pocket for
stuffing. Brush well with melted butter;
salt and pepper, and stuff pocket.

Melt remaining ¼ cup butter in a shallow
baking pan. Place fish in pan: do not overlap.
Cover and bake at 375° for 25 minutes, or
until fish flakes easily with a fork. Remove cover;
bake another 5 minutes. Yield: 4 servings.

FRIED FISH

2 pounds fish (fillets, steaks, or pan-dressed)
1 teaspoon salt
  Dash pepper
1 egg, slightly beaten
1 tablespoon milk or water
1 cup bread crumbs, cracker crumbs, cornmeal,
  or all-purpose flour
  Salad oil

Cut fish into serving-size portions. Sprinkle
both sides with salt and pepper. Combine beaten
egg and milk. Dip fish into egg mixture and roll in
crumbs. Place fish in heavy skillet containing
about ⅛ inch of hot salad oil. Fry at a moderate
heat. When fish is brown on one side, turn
carefully and brown the other side. Cooking time
should be about 10 minutes, depending on the
thickness of the fish. Drain on absorbent
paper. Yield: 6 servings.

OVEN-FRIED GROUPER

2 pounds grouper fillets or other fish fillets
1 tablespoon salt
1 cup milk
1 cup bread crumbs
4 tablespoons butter or margarine, melted

Cut fillets into serving-size portions. Add the salt to the milk, dip fish in milk and roll in crumbs; place in a well-greased baking pan. Pour melted butter over fish. Place pan on shelf near the top of a very hot oven and bake at 500° for 10 to 12 minutes, or until fish flakes easily with a fork. Watch fish carefully as it cooks. Serve immediately on a hot platter, plain or with a sauce. Yield: 6 servings.

WATER'S EDGE FISH FRY

Fresh, dressed fish
Salt and pepper to taste
Commercial pancake mix
1 egg, beaten with 1 tablespoon water
Margarine for frying
Lemon wedges for garnish

Dry fish on paper towels. Salt and pepper lightly on both sides. Coat with pancake mix; dip in egg and water mixture and then in pancake mix again. Heat margarine in skillet and fry fish until done and brown, turning once until fish flakes easily with a fork. Serve with lemon wedges.

MARINATED SPANISH MACKEREL FILLETS

2 pounds Spanish mackerel fillets or other fish fillets, fresh or frozen
½ cup vinegar
¼ cup melted margarine or salad oil
¼ cup freshly squeezed lemon juice
2 tablespoons grated lemon rind
1 tablespoon liquid smoke
1 tablespoon brown sugar
2 teaspoons salt
½ teaspoon Worcestershire sauce
2 bay leaves
Dash white pepper
Dash hot pepper sauce

Thaw fillets if frozen. Combine remaining ingredients and heat until mixture comes to the boiling point. Cool. Cut fillets into serving-size portions and place in a single layer in a shallow baking dish. Pour sauce over fish and let stand for 30 minutes, turning once. Remove fish, reserving sauce for basting. Place fish in well-greased, hinged wire grills. Cook about 4 inches from moderately hot coals for 8 minutes. Baste with remaining sauce. Turn and cook for 7 to 10 minutes longer, or until fish flakes easily with a fork. Yield: 6 servings.

FISH LOAF

2 cups cooked fish, skinned, boned, and flaked
1 egg
¼ cup milk
¾ cup·bread crumbs
½ teaspoon salt
¼ teaspoon pepper
1 tablespoon freshly squeezed lemon juice
3 tablespoons parsley
3 tablespoons chopped green pepper
Tomato Curry Sauce

Put fish in large bowl. Combine remaining ingredients and add to fish. Place mixture in greased loafpan. Bake at 350° for 45 minutes. Serve hot with Tomato Curry Sauce. Yield: 4 to 6 servings.

Tomato Curry Sauce
1 (6-ounce) can tomato paste
¾ cup water
1 onion
1 apple
1 clove garlic
1 bay leaf
1 teaspoon curry powder
2 tablespoons butter or margarine
2 teaspoons salt
½ teaspoon ground ginger

Heat tomato paste and water. Chop the onion and apple and crush garlic and bay leaf. Add these and remaining ingredients to tomato sauce. Simmer for 20 minutes. Strain. Yield: about 1¼ cups.

EASY GRILLED FISH

4 pounds assorted pan fish (small)
1 cup olive oil
1 teaspoon salt
½ teaspoon pepper
3 tablespoons freshly squeezed lime or lemon juice
1 tablespoon dried salad dressing mix (optional)
Lime or lemon slices for garnish

Clean, wash, and dry fish, leaving heads and tails on. Mix other ingredients and pour over fish. Let stand at room temperature in marinade for several hours. When ready to cook, remove from marinade. Place fish in hinged broiler. Close together, and broil over coals for 15 minutes on each side, or until fish is done. Brush during cooking with marinade and serve with lime or lemon slices. Yield: 6 servings.

Note: to oven broil, place fish in broiler pan. Combine other ingredients and pour over fish. Broil in oven until brown, turning once.

MARINATED REDFISH

1 pound redfish fillets or other fish fillets, fresh or fresh-frozen
½ cup soy sauce
2 tablespoons freshly squeezed lemon juice
2 cloves garlic, minced
¼ teaspoon ground ginger
1 teaspoon Worcestershire sauce
  Salt
  Pepper
  Dash ground cinnamon

Place fish fillets in a shallow baking dish. Combine soy sauce, lemon juice, garlic, ginger, and Worcestershire sauce. Pour over fish and let soak in the dish in refrigerator for 2 hours or overnight. Do not drain. Remove from refrigerator, sprinkle with salt, pepper, and cinnamon. Bake at 350° for approximately 20 minutes, or until fish flakes easily with a fork. Yield: 2 servings.

Note: If baking dish is not temperature-proof, bring to room temperature before placing in oven.

GRILLED PERCH FILLETS

2 pounds perch fillets or other fish fillets, fresh or frozen
½ cup salad oil
⅓ cup freshly squeezed lemon juice
¼ cup chopped onion
2 tablespoons capers and juice
2 tablespoons catsup
1 tablespoon salt
2 teaspoons sugar
2 teaspoons Worcestershire sauce
4 bay leaves, crushed
2 cloves garlic, finely chopped
¼ teaspoon pepper
  Paprika

Thaw fillets if frozen. Cut into serving-size portions. Place in a single layer in a shallow baking pan. Combine remaining ingredients, except paprika. Pour sauce over fish and let stand for 30 minutes, turning once. Remove fish, reserving sauce for basting. Place fish in well-greased, hinged wire grills. Sprinkle with paprika. Cook on a barbecue grill about 4 inches from moderately hot coals for 8 minutes. Baste with remaining sauce and sprinkle with paprika. Turn and cook for 7 to 10 minutes longer, or until fish flakes easily with a fork. Yield: 6 servings.

PERCH JAMBALAYA

1 pound perch fillets or other fish fillets, fresh or frozen
½ cup chopped bacon
1 cup chopped onion
½ cup chopped green pepper
1 clove garlic, finely chopped
1 chicken bouillon cube
1 cup boiling water
1 (1-pound) can tomatoes
1 (8-ounce) can tomato sauce
1 cup uncooked regular rice
¼ cup chopped parsley
1 teaspoon salt
¼ teaspoon thyme
  Dash ground cloves
  Dash ground nutmeg
  Dash cayenne pepper

Thaw fillets if frozen. Skin fillets and cut into 1-inch pieces. Cook bacon until crisp. Add onion, green pepper, and garlic, and cook until tender. Dissolve bouillon cube in boiling water. Combine all ingredients and pour into a well-greased 2-quart casserole dish. Cover and bake at 350° for 50 to 60 minutes, or until rice is tender and fish flakes easily with a fork. Yield: 6 servings.

PERCH KABOBS

2 pounds yellow perch fillets or other fish fillets, fresh or frozen
⅓ cup French dressing
3 large, firm tomatoes
1 (1-pound) can whole potatoes, drained
1½ teaspoons salt
  Dash pepper
⅓ cup melted shortening or salad oil

Thaw fillets if frozen. Skin fillets and cut into strips approximately 1 inch wide by 4 inches long. Place fish in a shallow baking dish. Pour dressing over fish and let stand for 30 minutes. Wash tomatoes. Remove stem ends and cut into sixths. Remove fish, reserving dressing. Roll fillets and place on skewers alternately with potatoes and tomatoes. Place kabobs on a well-greased broiler pan. Add salt, pepper, and remaining dressing to melted shortening; mix thoroughly. Brush kabobs with seasoned mixture. Broil about 3 inches from source of heat for 4 to 6 minutes. Turn kabobs carefully and brush with shortening. Broil 4 to 6 minutes longer, or until fish flakes easily with a fork. Yield: 6 servings.

POMPANO EN PAPILLOTE

    1 lemon, sliced
    1 bay leaf
    1 sprig thyme
    6 pompano fillets
    3 cups boiling salted water
    2 tablespoons butter or margarine
    3 tablespoons all-purpose flour
    1 onion, minced
 1½ cups fish stock
    1 cup cooked shrimp, chopped
   ½ cup crabmeat
   ½ cup mushroom pieces
   ¼ teaspoon salt
    2 egg yolks, beaten

Add lemon slices, bay leaf, thyme, and fillets to the boiling salted water. Simmer for 15 minutes. Remove fillets, open flat, and place each on individual sheet of parchment paper or greased brown paper. Melt butter in another saucepan over medium heat. Add flour and onion; stir and brown lightly. Add fish stock. Cook until sauce thickens, about 5 to 6 minutes. Stir in shrimp, crabmeat, mushrooms, and salt. Remove from heat and stir in egg yolks. Spoon sauce over fillets. Fold paper to form a case around each fillet. Bake at 400° for 10 minutes. To serve, split and fold back each casement. Yield: 6 servings.

FISH PUDDING

    3 pounds bluefish, boned and skinned
   ½ teaspoon garlic salt
   ½ teaspoon pepper
   ½ teaspoon mace
   ½ cup butter or margarine
    1 tablespoon shortening
    1 (8-ounce) can tomato sauce
    1 medium onion, chopped
    1 green pepper, chopped
   ¼ cup chopped celery
   12 salted crackers, crushed
    1 cup milk
    4 eggs, beaten

Grind, or finely chop, the fish. Add garlic salt, pepper, and mace. Melt butter and shortening over medium heat; stir in tomato sauce. Add onion, pepper, and celery. Cook until onion is transparent and remove from heat. Stir in fish, crackers, milk, and eggs. Pour into a 3-quart casserole dish. Cover and bake at 350° for 1 hour and 15 minutes. Yield: 8 servings.

HOT SEAFOOD SALAD

    1 medium onion, chopped
    1 green pepper, chopped
    1 cup sliced celery
   ½ pound crabmeat, fresh or canned
   ¾ pound cooked shrimp
   ½ teaspoon salt
   ¼ teaspoon pepper
    1 cup mayonnaise
    2 tablespoons melted butter or margarine
   ½ cup bread crumbs

Combine all ingredients except the butter and bread crumbs. Place in a greased 1½-quart casserole dish. Blend butter with bread crumbs and sprinkle over top of casserole. Bake at 350° for 30 minutes. Yield: 4 to 6 servings.

MOLDED FISH SALAD

    2 tablespoons plain gelatin
   ¼ cup cold water
 1½ cups tomato soup
    1 link American cheese food
    1 cup shredded crabmeat, shrimp, or tuna
   ½ cup diced celery
   ½ cup diced green pepper
    1 tablespoon grated onion
    1 tablespoon vinegar
   ⅛ teaspoon dry mustard
    1 teaspoon salt
    1 cup mayonnaise

Soak gelatin in cold water. Add to hot tomato soup and set aside to cool. Blend in cheese food, cut into pieces, and allow to soften. Mix fish, celery, pepper, onion, and seasoning with mayonnaise and add to soup mixture when slightly congealed. Spoon into a 1-quart mold and chill until firm. Yield: 6 servings.

SARDINE-CHEESE TOASTWICH

    2 (3¾- or 4-ounce) cans sardines in mustard
      sauce
    2 tablespoons butter or margarine, softened
    6 slices bread
    6 slices cheese
      Paprika

Drain sardines and reserve sauce. Split sardines in half lengthwise. Combine butter and 1 teaspoon sardine mustard sauce. Spread bread with mustard-butter. Place sardines on bread and cover with cheese. Sprinkle with paprika. Place sandwiches on a cookie sheet, 15 x 12 inches. Bake at 450° for 8 to 10 minutes, or until cheese melts. Yield: 6 servings.

DANDY FISH SANDWICH

6 (2½- to 3-ounce) raw breaded fish portions
2 tablespoons melted shortening or salad oil
   Paprika
6 slices toasted, buttered bread
   Mushroom Topping

Place frozen fish portions on a well-greased cookie sheet. Drizzle melted shortening over fish. Sprinkle with paprika. Bake at 500° for 10 to 15 minutes, or until fish is brown and flakes easily with a fork. Place toast on a cookie sheet. Place a fish portion on each piece of toast. Top each portion with approximately ⅓ cup Mushroom Topping. Broil about 3 inches from source of heat for 4 to 6 minutes, or until lightly browned and topping is set. Yield: 6 servings.

Mushroom Topping

2 (4-ounce) cans mushroom stems and pieces, drained
2 tablespoons melted shortening
1 cup grated cheese
⅔ cup chopped tomatoes
2 eggs, beaten
1 teaspoon salt
   Dash pepper

Chop mushrooms. Cook in shortening until lightly browned. Add to remaining ingredients and mix thoroughly. Yield: about 2 cups.

EASY TOMATO SURPRISE SALAD

2 (3¾- or 4-ounce) cans sardines
¾ cup sliced celery
2 hard-cooked eggs, chopped
¼ cup mayonnaise or salad dressing
2 tablespoons chopped ripe olives
2 teaspoons freshly squeezed lemon juice
1 teaspoon prepared mustard
½ teaspoon salt
   Dash pepper
6 medium tomatoes
   Salad greens

Drain sardines and cut into large pieces. Combine celery, eggs, mayonnaise, olives, lemon juice, mustard, salt, and pepper. Add sardines and toss lightly. Chill. Cut each tomato into 5 or 6 sections almost to stem end and spread apart slightly. Fill each tomato with sardine salad. Serve on salad greens. Yield: 6 servings.

SARDINE ANTIPASTO

3 (3¾- or 4-ounce) cans sardines
2 (4-ounce) cans button mushrooms
   Marinade
   Lettuce
   Celery sticks
   Cucumber slices
   Green pepper rings
   Olives
   Radish roses
   Tomato wedges
   Italian dressing

Drain sardines and mushrooms. Place in a shallow baking dish. Pour Marinade over sardines and mushrooms; let stand in refrigerator for 30 minutes. Drain. Have remaining ingredients well chilled. Cover a large platter or tray with lettuce. Arrange all ingredients, except dressing, attractively on lettuce. Serve with Italian dressing. Yield: 6 servings.

Marinade

½ cup French dressing
¼ cup soy sauce
2 tablespoons wine vinegar
1 clove garlic, crushed
   Dash ground ginger
   Dash pepper

Combine all ingredients. Add enough water to make 1 cup of marinade; mix thoroughly.

SARDINE SALAD PLATTER

1 (8-ounce) can sardines
4 hard-cooked eggs
½ teaspoon prepared mustard
1 teaspoon salt
   Dash pepper
1 teaspoon celery seed
2 teaspoons Worcestershire sauce
6 tablespoons salad oil
5 tablespoons vinegar
2 tablespoons chopped parsley
2 tablespoons chopped green onions
   Lettuce leaves
4 cups shredded lettuce
1 cup sliced celery

Drain sardines and reserve oil. Mash 1 egg yolk and combine with sardine oil. Add seasonings, salad oil, vinegar, parsley, onions, and 1 chopped egg white. Blend thoroughly. Arrange lettuce leaves as cups on plate. Combine shredded lettuce and celery and place in lettuce cups.

Slice the 3 remaining egg whites and arrange with sardines on top of lettuce. Pour dressing over salad. Yield: 6 servings.

SHAD ROE AND BACON

1½ **pounds shad roe or other fish roe,**
   fresh or frozen
 ½ **teaspoon salt**
   Dash pepper
12 **slices bacon**

Thaw roe if frozen. Drain on absorbent paper. Sprinkle with salt and pepper. Fry bacon until crisp in a 10-inch frying pan; drain on absorbent paper. Fry roe in hot bacon fat at moderate heat for 3 to 5 minutes, or until brown. Turn carefully and fry 3 to 5 minutes longer, or until brown. Drain on absorbent paper. Serve with bacon. Yield: 6 servings.

BROILED SHAD ROE

2 **shad roe**
   Salted water
   Juice of ½ lemon
   Cold water
4 **tablespoons butter**
   Salt and pepper to taste
1 **teaspoon white wine vinegar**
1 **tablespoon chopped parsley**
   Crisp bacon
   Scrambled eggs

Simmer shad roe 15 minutes in salted water to cover, with lemon juice. Remove with slotted spatula. Transfer to cold water for 5 minutes, drain, and pat dry.

Melt butter in a saucepan, sprinkle roe with salt and pepper, place on a greased rack, and brush surface with butter. Broil approximately 4 inches from flame for 5 minutes. Turn, and again brush with butter.

Broil until surface is a light golden brown. Place on serving platter or plates. Cook remaining butter in saucepan over high heat until it turns quite dark. Stir in vinegar and parsley. Pour over shad roe and serve with crisp bacon and scrambled eggs. Yield: 2 servings.

RED SNAPPER EN PAPILLOTE

2 **pounds red snapper fillets or other fish**
   fillets, fresh or frozen
1 **teaspoon salt**
   Dash pepper
½ **cup butter or margarine, melted**
2 **tablespoons chopped parsley**
1 **tablespoon freshly squeezed lemon juice**
1 **teaspoon salt**
½ **teaspoon chopped dillweed**
6 **thin onion slices**
1½ **cups thinly sliced carrots**
1 **(8-ounce) package sliced Swiss cheese**

Thaw fillets if frozen. Skin fillets and cut into serving-size portions. Sprinkle fish on both sides with salt and pepper. Combine butter, parsley, lemon juice, salt, and dillweed. Cut 6 (12-inch) squares of heavy-duty aluminum foil. Grease lightly. Place 1 teaspoon parsley butter on one half of each square of foil. Place fish on butter. Separate onion slices into rings and place on fish. Top with ¼ cup carrot slices. Pour remaining parsley butter over carrots, dividing evenly among 6 packages. Top each serving with a slice of cheese. Fold foil over cheese and seal edges by making double folds in the foil. Place packages on a baking pan. Bake at 400° for 35 to 40 minutes, or until fish flakes easily with a fork and vegetables are cooked. To serve, cut around edges of package and fold the foil back. Yield: 6 servings.

LEMON-BUTTER GRILLED
RED SNAPPER FILLETS

2 **pounds red snapper fillets or other fish fillets,**
   fresh or frozen
½ **cup butter or margarine, melted**
2 **tablespoons freshly squeezed lemon juice**
1 **tablespoon chopped parsley**
1 **tablespoon hickory liquid smoke**
2 **teaspoons salt**
   Dash pepper

Thaw fillets if frozen. Cut into serving-size portions. Combine remaining ingredients. Baste fish with sauce. Place fish in well-greased, hinged wire grills. Cook on a barbecue grill about 4 inches from moderately hot coals for 8 minutes. Baste with remaining sauce. Turn and cook for 7 to 10 minutes longer, or until fish flakes easily with a fork. Yield: 6 servings.

RED SNAPPER PARMESAN

2 pounds red snapper fillets or other fish,
  fresh or frozen
1 cup commercial sour cream
¼ cup grated Parmesan cheese
1 tablespoon freshly squeezed lemon juice
1 tablespoon grated onion
½ teaspoon salt
  Dash hot pepper sauce
  Paprika

Thaw frozen fillets. Skin fillets and cut into
serving-size portions. Place in a single layer in a
well-greased 12- x 8- x 2-inch baking dish.
Combine remaining ingredients except paprika.
Spread sour cream mixture over fish. Sprinkle
with paprika. Bake at 350° for 25 to 30 minutes,
or until fish flakes easily with a fork.
Yield: 6 servings.

BOUILLABAISSE — FLORIDA STYLE

2 pounds red snapper, mullet, or redfish fillets,
  fresh or frozen
1 pound raw shrimp, fresh or frozen
1 (12-ounce) can fresh or frozen oysters
1 cup coarsely chopped onion
1 clove garlic, finely chopped
½ cup butter, margarine, or olive oil
3 tablespoons all-purpose flour
1 cup coarsely chopped fresh tomatoes
2 cups fish stock or water
1 cup tomato juice
½ cup sherry
½ lemon, sliced
2 teaspoons salt
⅛ teaspoon cayenne pepper
⅛ teaspoon leaf thyme
3 whole allspice
1 small bay leaf
  Pinch saffron (optional)
  French bread

Thaw fish if frozen. Skin fillets and cut into
slices or large chunks. Thaw shrimp if frozen.
Peel, devein, and wash shrimp. Thaw oysters if
frozen. Set aside. Sauté onion and garlic in butter
in Dutch oven until tender. Blend in flour. Add
remaining ingredients except French bread; mix.
Simmer gently for 30 minutes, or until flavors are
well blended. Add fish, shrimp, and oysters.
Simmer gently for 15 to 20 minutes, or until
shrimp are tender and fish flakes easily with a
fork. Serve with crusty French bread.
Yield: 10 cups, or about 8 servings.

HEARTY BOUILLABAISSE

1 leek, chopped (optional)
1 onion, chopped
2 cloves garlic, minced
2 chopped tomatoes
½ cup olive oil
2 pounds fish, snapper, grouper, or snook
2 pounds shellfish, lobster, crab, shrimp, or
  scallops
2 teaspoons chopped parsley
  Salt, pepper, paprika, saffron, and bay leaf
1 quart fish stock
1 cup white wine

Sauté leek, onion, garlic, and tomatoes in oil.
Add fish, shellfish, parsley, and seasonings. Cover
all with fish stock or boiling water. Simmer for 10
minutes, adding wine during last 5 minutes.
Yield: 8 servings.

COURT-BOUILLON OF REDFISH

1 (6-pound) redfish
¼ cup shortening
¼ cup all-purpose flour
2 large onions, sliced
1 (1-pound) can tomatoes
2 bay leaves
¼ teaspoon ground allspice
1 teaspoon salt
4 green peppers, chopped
4 green onions and tops, chopped
1 clove garlic, minced
1 cup water
2 thin slices lemon
1 teaspoon minced parsley
1 cup claret wine

Slice redfish across the backbone in 3-inch-
wide slices. Make a roux by cooking shortening
and flour until dark brown. Add onions and sauté
until tender. Add tomatoes; cook for 5 minutes.
Add remaining ingredients with the exception of
the wine and fish; simmer for 30 minutes. Add
fish and continue to simmer for 20 minutes. Add
wine, bring to boil, and serve. Yield: 8 servings.

TROUT ITALIANO

6 pan-dressed trout
½ cup tomato sauce
2 (¾-ounce) packages garlic-cheese salad
  dressing mix
2 tablespoons salad oil
2 tablespoons chopped parsley
2 tablespoons grated Parmesan cheese

Clean, wash, and dry fish. Combine remaining ingredients, except cheese. Brush fish inside and out with sauce. Place in a thoroughly greased, 13- x 9- x 2-inch baking dish. Brush with remaining sauce, and sprinkle with cheese. Let stand for 30 minutes. Bake at 350° for 25 to 30 minutes, or until fish flakes easily with a fork. Turn oven control to broil. Place fish about 3 inches from source of heat and broil for 1 to 2 minutes, or until crisp and lightly browned. Yield: 6 servings.

PICCADILLY TROUT

    2 pounds pan-dressed trout or other small pan-dressed fish, fresh or frozen
 1½ teaspoons salt
  ¼ teaspoon pepper
    Dash paprika
  ½ cup butter or margarine
    2 teaspoons chopped dillweed
    3 tablespoons freshly squeezed lemon juice

Thaw fish if frozen; or clean and cut the fresh catch almost through lengthwise and spread open. Sprinkle with salt and pepper. Dust with paprika. Melt butter in a 10-inch frying pan; add dillweed. Place fish in a single layer, flesh side down, in the hot dill butter.

Fry at moderate heat for 2 to 3 minutes. Turn carefully. Fry 2 to 3 minutes longer, or until fish flakes easily with a fork. Place on a warm serving platter. Keep warm.

When all the fish have been fried, turn heat very low and stir in lemon juice. Pour sauce over fish. Yield: 6 servings.

GRILLED TROUT WITH SESAME SEED

    6 pan-dressed trout or other small fish, fresh or frozen
  ¼ cup salad oil, butter, or margarine, melted
  ¼ cup sesame seed
 1½ tablespoons freshly squeezed lemon juice
  ½ teaspoon salt
    Dash pepper

Thaw fish if frozen. Clean, wash, and dry fish. Combine remaining ingredients. Place fish in well-greased, hinged wire grills. Baste fish with sauce. Cook on a barbecue grill about 4 inches from moderately hot coals for 5 to 8 minutes. Baste with remaining sauce. Turn and cook 5 to 8 minutes longer, or until fish flakes easily with a fork. Yield: 6 servings.

TROUT IN WINE SAUCE

    6 pan-dressed trout or other fish
    1 cup dry white wine
  ½ cup melted shortening or salad oil
    1 (4-ounce) can mushroom stems and pieces, drained
  ¼ cup chopped green onions
    2 tablespoons freshly squeezed lemon juice
    2 tablespoons chopped parsley
    2 teaspoons salt
  ¼ teaspoon crushed bay leaves
  ¼ teaspoon pepper
  ¼ teaspoon thyme

Clean, wash and dry fish. Cut 6 (18-inch-square) pieces of heavy-duty aluminum foil. Grease lightly. Place fish on foil. Combine remaining ingredients; pour sauce over fish. Bring the foil up over the fish and close all edges with tight double folds. Place packages on a grill about 6 inches from moderately hot coals. Cook for 20 to 25 minutes, or until fish flakes easily with a fork. Yield: 4 to 6 servings.

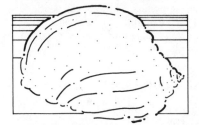

STUFFED TROUT

    2 pounds dressed trout, or other fresh fish
    1 clove garlic, crushed
    Juice of 1 lemon
  ¼ cup water
    Dash thyme
    1 bay leaf
  ½ pound fresh or canned mushrooms, thinly sliced
  ¼ cup chopped onion
    5 stalks celery, thinly sliced
    1 large tomato, peeled and quartered
    Dash pepper

Clean, wash, and dry fish. Place fish in a well-greased shallow baking dish; rub with crushed garlic and lemon juice. Add water, thyme, and bay leaf. Bake at 400° for 30 minutes. Combine mushrooms, onion, celery, tomato, and pepper in a saucepan; cook for 8 to 10 minutes, or until liquid has evaporated. Fill cooked fish with this mixture and return to oven for several minutes. Yield: 4 servings.

CIOPPINO

2 cloves garlic, minced
1 large onion, chopped
1 green pepper, diced
2 carrots, grated
2 tablespoons olive oil
¼ cup chopped parsley
1 (28-ounce) can tomatoes
2 bay leaves
2 teaspoons salt
½ teaspoon seasoned pepper
4 drops hot pepper sauce
2 cups clam juice or fish broth
1 pound shrimp, frozen and cleaned
1 (6½-ounce) can crabmeat
1 cup oysters, fresh or canned
½ pound fillet of sole, fresh or frozen,
    cut into 1-inch pieces

Sauté garlic, onion, green pepper, and carrots in olive oil in a 3-quart saucepan for 3 to 5 minutes. Add parsley, tomatoes, bay leaves, salt, pepper, hot pepper sauce, and clam juice or fish broth. Cook and simmer for 15 minutes. Add shrimp, crabmeat, oysters, and sole, and continue cooking for 15 more minutes. Serve at once, steaming hot, from a large tureen, or in individual extra-large soup bowls. Yield: 6 servings.

SPECIAL SEAFOOD GUMBO

1½ to 2 pounds fresh shrimp
½ teaspoon crab boil
2 tablespoons bacon drippings
2 tablespoons flour
1 large onion, finely chopped
1 cup cooked, chopped ham
2 pounds fresh okra, washed, stemmed, and
    chopped, or 1 (10-ounce) box frozen okra,
    chopped
3 stalks celery, chopped
2 tablespoons chopped parsley
1 (16-ounce) can tomatoes
1 large green pepper, chopped
1 pound crabmeat, fresh or frozen, picked
    from the shell
1 clove garlic, mashed
1 teaspoon salt
½ teaspoon freshly ground pepper
¼ teaspoon dried thyme
¼ teaspoon ground oregano
2 bay leaves
    Cooked rice

Cover well-washed shrimp with water and add crab boil. Cook until shrimp are tender, about 10 minutes. Drain and save the water. Peel shrimp. Make a roux with bacon drippings and flour in an iron pot or Dutch oven. Add the chopped onion and sauté until transparent. Add ham and okra. Cook about 10 minutes over medium heat, stirring constantly. Add the shrimp water, celery, parsley, tomatoes, green pepper, crabmeat, garlic, salt, and pepper. Simmer mixture for an hour. Add thyme, oregano, bay leaves, and peeled shrimp. Cook for an additional 20 minutes. Serve over fluffy rice. This gumbo can be frozen. Yield: 8 to 10 servings.

Filé Gumbo: Filé can be substituted for the okra. Add 1 teaspoon filé just before serving. Do not reheat!

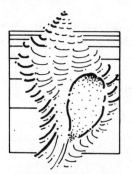

SWEET-SOUR FISH

2 to 3 pounds trout
3 cups boiling water
1 onion, sliced
1 tablespoon chopped celery
1 tablespoon chopped parsley
1 carrot, sliced
6 peppercorns
2 teaspoons salt
½ cup firmly packed brown sugar
¼ cup vinegar
¼ cup seedless raisins
10 whole cloves
1 lemon, sliced
1 onion, sliced
8 to 10 gingersnaps, crushed
    Ring of cooked rice

Clean trout and leave whole or slice thick. Bring to a boil 3 cups water with onion, celery, parsley, carrot, peppercorns, and salt. Place fish on a rack and let steam for at least 10 minutes. Remove from stock; strain stock and set aside. Mix brown sugar, vinegar, raisins, and whole cloves; add to strained fish stock. Add sliced lemon and onion and boil about 10 minutes. Add slices of cooked fish and crushed gingersnaps and heat thoroughly in sauce. Serve in center of ring of cooked rice. Yield: 4 to 6 servings.

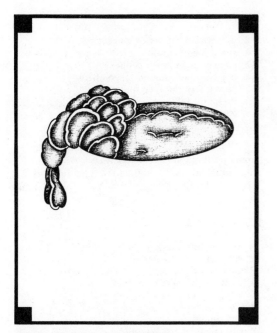

DIPS & SAUCES

Many fish and seafood dishes are cooked in sauces, or have spices and herbs added later for flavoring, Seafood, especially, is often used for cocktails. Sauces for shrimp, lobster, or crab cocktails may range from the mild to the very hot and spicy.

Poached, fried, or baked fish and shellfish can always be improved with the right sauce or dip.

The recipes on the following pages are very simple. A versatile cook can improvise on our suggestions, increasing or decreasing a given amount of seasoning at will. In fact, culinary experimentation is encouraged.

TOMATO SAUCE

    2 cups canned tomatoes
    2 tablespoons butter or margarine
    2 tablespoons all-purpose flour
    1 teaspoon Worcestershire sauce
    ½ teaspoon salt
    ¼ teaspoon pepper

Cook tomatoes for 10 minutes and strain to remove seeds. Melt butter, stir in flour, and add hot strained tomatoes and seasonings. Cook until sauce thickens. Yield: 6 servings.

SPICY DUNK SAUCE

    ½ cup chili sauce
    ¼ cup well-drained bottled horseradish
    1 teaspoon Worcestershire sauce
    1 teaspoon minced onion
    ¼ teaspoon garlic salt
    ½ teaspoon salt
    ⅛ teaspoon pepper
    1 tablespoon vinegar
    2 dashes hot pepper sauce
    ¼ teaspoon commercial meat sauce
    1 teaspoon celery seed
    2 tablespoons sugar
    1 teaspoon celery salt

Combine all ingredients. Keep in a covered jar in the refrigerator 2 or 3 days before using, to blend flavors thoroughly. Yield: about ¾ cup.

SEAFOOD DIP

    1 cup flaked or canned fish
    2 (3-ounce) packages cream cheese
    ⅓ cup chopped stuffed olives
    ¼ cup mayonnaise or salad dressing
    3 tablespoons half-and-half
    ¼ teaspoon grated onion
    2 drops hot pepper sauce
       Potato chips
       Pretzel sticks
       Parsley

Drain canned fish. Reserve 6 pieces of fish for garnish. Soften cream cheese at room temperature. Add olives, mayonnaise, half-and-half, onion, hot pepper sauce, and fish; blend into a paste. Chill. Serve in a bowl surrounded by potato chips and pretzel sticks. Garnish dip with parsley and fish. Yield: about 1 pint.

SAUCE FOR SHRIMP, LOBSTER, CRABMEAT

    1 pint mayonnaise
    ½ cup India relish
    1 teaspoon chopped olives
    1 pimiento, chopped
    1 tablespoon prepared mustard
    1 tablespoon commercial meat sauce
    1 pint commercial chili sauce
    1 chopped hard-cooked egg
    ½ green pepper, chopped
    2 tablespoons chopped celery
       Salt and pepper to taste
       Dash paprika

Mix all ingredients; chill and serve. Yield: about 4¼ cups.

DRAWN BUTTER SAUCE

¼ cup butter
2 tablespoons all-purpose flour
½ teaspoon salt
⅛ teaspoon pepper
⅛ teaspoon paprika
1 cup water
1 teaspoon freshly squeezed lemon juice
2 tablespoons minced parsley (optional)

Melt butter in double boiler. Stir in flour, salt, pepper, and paprika. Slowly blend in the water and cook until thickened. Just before serving, stir in lemon juice. For extra color and flavor, add 2 tablespoons minced parsley. Serve with broiled or baked fish. Yield: 1¼ cups.

CHILI-MUSTARD SAUCE

¼ cup butter, margarine, or salad oil
¼ cup minced onion
1 clove garlic, minced
½ teaspoon salt
Dash pepper
1 teaspoon Worcestershire sauce
1 teaspoon prepared mustard
2 tablespoons chili sauce

Combine butter, onion, and garlic in a saucepan over low heat. Cook until onion is tender, about 10 minutes, stirring frequently to prevent browning. Add salt and rest of ingredients; mix well; heat. Yield: 4 servings.

LEMON PARSLEY SAUCE

½ cup butter or margarine, melted
1 teaspoon grated lemon rind
3 tablespoons freshly squeezed lemon juice
1 tablespoon chopped parsley

Combine all ingredients. Serve hot over fish. Yield: about ½ cup.

VATIER DIP

½ cup salad oil
2 tablespoons tarragon vinegar
1 teaspoon dry mustard
1 teaspoon prepared mustard
¼ teaspoon garlic salt
¼ cup finely chopped celery
2 green onions, including tops, minced

Mix all ingredients together; add salt and pepper to taste. Let stand for several hours. Serve hot or cold. Yield: 1¼ cups.

CREOLE SAUCE

2 tablespoons butter or margarine
¼ cup minced onion
⅓ cup chopped green pepper
¼ cup chopped, stuffed green olives
1½ cups finely chopped tomatoes
¼ teaspoon salt
1 teaspoon sugar
Dash cayenne pepper

Melt butter in a skillet. Sauté onion and green pepper until onion is lightly browned. Add remaining ingredients; simmer 10 to 15 minutes. Serve over broiled or baked fish. Yield: about 2 cups.

REMOULADE SAUCE

4 tablespoons horseradish
½ cup tarragon vinegar
2 tablespoons catsup
1 tablespoon paprika
1 teaspoon salt
1 clove garlic
1 cup salad oil
½ cup chopped green onions
½ cup chopped celery
½ teaspoon cayenne pepper

Place all ingredients in blender and blend thoroughly. To serve, allow boiled shrimp to marinate in sauce for about 4 hours. Yield: about 2 cups.

HURRICANE SAUCE

4 tablespoons dry mustard
2 tablespoons dried horseradish
2 tablespoons wine vinegar
6 tablespoons olive oil
1 tablespoon paprika
1 tablespoon turmeric
½ teaspoon white pepper
½ teaspoon salt
2 tablespoons chopped hearts of celery
2 tablespoons finely chopped onion
1 tablespoon chopped parsley

Mix mustard and horseradish. Blend with enough water to make a smooth consistency that will pour. Let the mixture stand for 15 or 20 minutes, adding extra water if necessary.

In a separate bowl, blend vinegar, oil, paprika, turmeric, white pepper, and salt. Add horseradish and mustard mixture, celery, and onion. Just before serving, add parsley. Serve over ice-cold boiled shrimp on a bed of shredded lettuce. Yield: 4 servings.